ROYAL CITIES OF
THE ANCIENT MAYA

ROYAL CITIES OF THE ANCIENT MAYA

Thames & Hudson

MICHAEL D. COE   PHOTOGRAPHS BY BARRY BRUKOFF

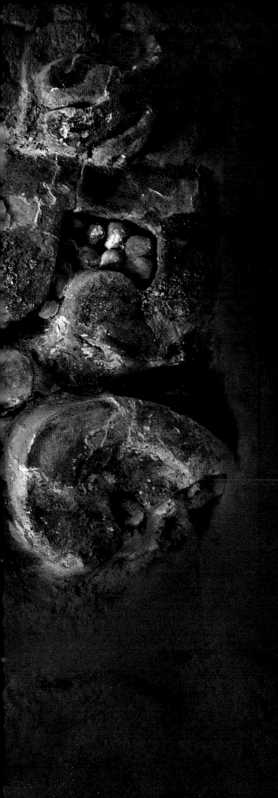

CONTENTS

I dedicate this book to my granddaughter, Lea Marina Brukoff, who at her tender age is already an inveterate traveler.

PHOTOGRAPHER'S NOTE

When Mike Coe and I discussed the general direction to take in creating *Royal Cities of the Ancient Maya*, we agreed that I should attempt to provide a photographic equivalent of English artist Frederick Catherwood's renowned drawings and lithographs of the Maya world in the 1850s. He traveled on mule back and carried a *camera lucida*, which allowed him to accurately trace the complex forms of Maya architecture for his meticulously detailed works. Digital-era advancements have enabled me to composite many of the photographs in a way that would have been impossible in an earlier age.

There are a number of images in the book that present views of sites that cannot be seen even by visitors to those sites. The stucco frieze at El Mirador (pages 24–25), for instance, was photographed under extremely difficult conditions, as the upper and lower rows of the frieze were separated by workmen's scaffolding. I had to shoot many individual images and meticulously piece them together, absent the scaffolding. The 56-foot-long Balamk'u frieze (gatefold front between pages 56 and 57) is composited from ten photographs. It is impossible to photograph the entire frieze in a single shot, because one can stand no more than 8 feet away from it. The white stucco frieze on the Acropolis summit at Ek' Balam (pages 186–87) is also a composite, as many wooden columns support the thatched roof, precluding a clear shot. And each of the photos that form the composite had to be taken at an odd angle; then their frontal perspectives had to be aligned and composited to create the finished image. No archaeologist has ever seen this frieze as it appears in this book. The photo of the three pyramids at the summit of the La Danta temple-pyramid, glimpsed through thick tropical foliage (pages 18–19), is, in fact, three separate photographs blended into a panorama to convey the feeling of the pyramids emerging from the dense jungle. The actual jungle vegetation was too thick to capture this sensation in one photograph. The other panoramic images in the book were created in a similar fashion.

Almost all ancient cultures were in awe of the sun and the moon and created rituals and made sacrifices to ensure the continued existence of those potent and incomprehensible forces of nature. I arranged my trips through the Maya empire to coincide with the full moon, which appears in a number of images, to acknowledge the extraordinary power that these elemental forces had on the Maya people.

What I hope this book will impart to the reader is a sense of how it feels to wander among the Maya ruins, to walk through the thick jungle and come upon these marvelous edifices. It is that sense of wonder that I have strived to capture in my photographs, presenting the ruins in a manner that emphasizes their beauty and the uniqueness of their architecture.

—Barry Brukoff

Cabo Catoche

Cancún

YUCATÁN

Mérida •   ◇ Ek' Balam

◇ Chichén Itzá

Mayapán ◇   ◇ Valladolid   ◇ Cobá

Isla Cozumel

Uxmal ◇   ◇ Kabah   ◇ Tulum

Sayil ◇◇ Labná   ◇ Muyil

Gulf of Mexico

Campeche ○

Edzná ◇   ◇ Tabasqueño   QUINTANA

◇ Hochob   ROO

CAMPECHE

Veracruz ○

Chicanná → ◇ Becán   ◇ Dzibanché

Ciudad   Balamk'u ◇ ◇ Xpuhil   ○ Chetumal
del Carmen   Hormiguero ◇   ◇ Kohunlich
    Escárcega ○   ◇ Río Bec

*Banco
Chinchorro*

Calakmul ◇

Ambergris Cay

TABASCO

VERACRUZ   Villahermosa ○   El Mirador ◇ ◇ Nakbé   Belize City ○

Caribbean

◇ San Bartolo

MEXICO   Palenque ◇   ◇ Tikal   *Belize* ○ Belmopan   *Turneffe
Islands*

Sea

Piedras Negras ◇   BELIZE

Usumacinta

Toniná ◇   Yaxchilán ◇   ○ Flores

Tuxtla   Bonampak ◇   *Pasión*
Gutiérrez ○

OAXACA   CHIAPAS   *Salinas*

Bay Islands

Puerto
Barrios ○

*Lago
de Izabal*   *Motagua*   ○ San Pedro Sula

GUATEMALA

Quiriguá ◇   HONDURAS

Pacific Ocean

Copán ◇

○ Guatemala City

EL
SALVADOR

○ Tegucigalpa

MAYA GENESIS

INTRODUCTION

A little over 170 years ago, two young explorers—the American lawyer and diplomat John Lloyd Stephens and the English topographical artist Frederick Catherwood—arrived at the ruins of the great Maya city of Copán, in Honduras. It was the height of the rainy season, and the fallen temples and toppled monuments were shrouded in dense, wet vegetation. As their local workmen began the task of clearing . . .

> we sat down on the very edge of the wall, and strove in vain to penetrate the mystery by which we were surrounded. Who were the people that built this city? In the ruined cities of Egypt, even in the long-lost Petra, the stranger knows the story of the people whose vestiges are around him. America, say historians, was peopled by savages; but savages never reared these structures, savages never carved these stones. We asked the Indians who made them, and their dull answer was "Quien sabe?" "who knows?"

Ek' Balam: view of the central plaza from the Acropolis (see pages 184–89).

In the course of their two great journeys in Yucatán, Guatemala, southeast Mexico, and Honduras, and in the magnificent volumes published by Stephens in 1841 and 1843, Stephens and Catherwood not only brought to light dozens of ruined cities but made it abundantly clear who had made them: the same Maya Indians that they had traveled among, and not Egyptians, lost tribes of Israel, Welshmen, or some other Old World people.

We now know a great deal about the Maya themselves. First of all, far from being near extinction (as some modern popular writers seem to believe), they are remarkably numerous: best estimates are that there are at least eight million people who speak one or another tongue belonging to the Mayan language family, most of them in northern Yucatán or in the highlands of Guatemala and Chiapas (Mexico). Many now live and work in the United States, part of a diaspora that resulted from a two-decade reign of terror conducted by the Guatemalan military from the late 1970s through the mid-1990s (some of the team washing your car might well be Maya). In the face of all sorts of repression, beginning of course with the long-drawn-out Spanish Conquest, their culture has been resilient as well as adaptable. In particular, the post-Conquest Maya have retained their religious vitality by melding native Maya beliefs and rituals with Catholic ones, so that it is often impossible to separate what is native from what is European.

Linguists have defined about twenty-nine or thirty distinct languages within the larger family, all of them as closely related to each other as, say, English is to other Germanic languages such as Dutch or Danish. While today they are mutually unintelligible, many thousands of years ago they were one; where this ancestral, proto-Mayan tongue was spoken is a mystery, but some think it may have been in the western Maya highlands of Guatemala and Chiapas. Nevertheless, the area occupied by Mayan speakers is remarkably homogenous: no other linguistic group (including the Aztecs) has ever managed to split up Maya territory in any lasting fashion.

MAYA CIVILIZATION TIME LINE

DATES CALIBRATED	PERIODS	SIGNIFICANT DEVELOPMENTS
1530		Spanish Conquest
	Late Postclassic	Tulum
		League of Mayapán
1200		
		Toltec hegemony in Yucatán
	Early Postclassic	Maya-Toltec Chichén Itzá
		Toltec arrive in Yucatán
925		
		Classic Maya collapse
	Terminal Classic	Río Bec, Chenes, Puuk cities
		Bonampak murals
800		
		Height of Maya civilization
	Late Classic	Reign of Janaab Pakal at Palenque
600		
		Teotihuacán interference and influence
	Early Classic	
250		First lowland Maya dated stela at Tikal
AD / BC	Late Preclassic	Massive pyramid-building in lowlands, San Bartolo
400		
	Middle Preclassic	
1000		Olmec civilization
	Early Preclassic	
1800		

As we shall see in this book, the Maya realm was many: there was never anything like a "Maya Empire," and even at the height of Maya civilization, numerous independent or quasi-independent city-states were scattered across the Maya region. One might therefore compare the Maya world to the small city-states of ancient Greece and Renaissance Italy. But in very recent decades, Maya hieroglyphic research has shown that Classic Maya elites were linked to each other by a high-status, literary language (and writing system) that was shared by all—in the way that medieval Latin, for instance, once bound together the elites and intellectuals of Europe, no matter what internecine wars and other mayhem were going on. And while each city-state had its own unique characteristics, all of them remained bound up in a common social and religious environment with very deep roots in the past.

MAYA ORIGINS

There is not one Maya area, but three. In the far north lies the relatively flat limestone shelf of the Petén-Yucatán Peninsula, which separates the Gulf of Mexico from the Caribbean. To its south are the volcano-studded highlands of Chiapas and Guatemala. And finally, there is the Pacific coastal plain.

As we now realize, the outer shell of our planet is made of a small number of enormous, rocky plates that are constantly in slow motion, pulling apart over the eons to form oceans, grinding together to form mountain chains; where one relatively heavy plate dips under a lighter one, volcanoes are formed, and earthquakes may devastate the landscape. This is the case for the highlands of Guatemala; here, in a country no bigger than Ohio, there are no fewer than twenty-nine volcanoes, nine of them active during the past two centuries. The soils are rich, and fields can be cultivated almost year round, with abundant yields of that Mesoamerican staple food, corn (maize), along with beans, peppers, squashes, and many other crops. One might therefore expect that Maya civilization first arose here, but that was not the case. As we shall see, fully settled village life began on the Pacific coastal plain to the south, and the apogee of ancient Maya culture took place to the north.

Driving south from Guatemala City to that coastal plain, one enters a different world, with temperatures that can only be called torrid. This is a mainly alluvial lowland, traversed by numerous rivers originating in the highlands. Today it is largely devoted to cattle ranching and enormous sugar plantations, but in the pre-Spanish past it was a land covered by maize fields and groves of cacao (the "chocolate tree"). Where the plain meets the sea there are mangrove-lined lagoons and estuaries that produce abundant fish and shellfish. It is in this environment that we have the first evidence of real villages, and the first Mesoamerican pottery and fired-clay figurines. Radiocarbon dates prove that this way of life had begun by at least 1800 BC, almost a millennium before the earliest known permanent settlements of the northern Maya area. One might expect these ancient peoples (dubbed "Mokaya" by archaeologists) to have been simple and unsophisticated, but their ceramics are some of the best ever manufactured in the New World, they already show social stratification, and we now know that they produced and drank chocolate!

THE OLMEC

Let us now cross the Isthmus of Tehuantepec to another coastal plain, this one lying along the Gulf of Mexico in the Mexican states of Veracruz and Tabasco. This is the homeland of the Olmec civilization, Mesoamerica's "mother culture," as many archaeologists (including me) believe. Here, as along the Pacific coast, rivers undulate across the landscape, flooding during the summer rains to cover natural river levees with annual deposits of rich mud. This is the most productive land for maize cultivation in all of the Americas.

About 1500 BC, San Lorenzo—Mesoamerica's first civilized center—took shape, atop a natural plateau raised by an underlying salt dome. Pottery from the deepest excavation levels on this site suggest that it might have been founded by Mokaya people from across the isthmus. Destroyed by unknown antagonists about 900 BC, San Lorenzo was under the rule of powerful chiefs—or, more likely, real kings—who could order gigantic portraits of themselves and have them set up in plazas, presumably in front of their thatch-roofed clay palaces. These are the famous colossal heads, enormous sculptures of basalt quarried on the slopes of a distant volcano and brought by raft and human labor to San Lorenzo.

Well before San Lorenzo's downfall, these people already had a complex religious system, which featured such deities as the gods of maize and rain, carved by expert

Monument 1, an Olmec colossal head from San Lorenzo, Veracruz. Early Preclassic, 1400–900 BC.

sculptors using a stone-on-stone technique (metallurgy was not to appear in Mesoamerica for another thousand years). During the time of San Lorenzo's ascendancy, the Maya of the lowlands to the east were nothing more than simple hunters, gatherers of wild plant foods, and small-scale cultivators; they knew nothing of such arts as pottery, let alone massive stone sculpture.

With the mysterious but total destruction of San Lorenzo, during which many dozens of huge stone monuments were defaced and/or smashed, another great Olmec center appeared well to its east: La Venta, situated on an island amid an extensive swamp just over the border between Veracruz and Tabasco. Occupied from about 900 to 400 BC, La Venta is noted for its 110-foot-high pyramid, for a large number of stone sculptures, some of them bearing complex relief scenes involving costumed individuals and gods, and for its magnificent jade offerings and ceremonial deposits. Excavations have shown that jade and other polished green stones were in use as far back as the Early Preclassic period (1800–900 BC) on the Pacific coast and in the Olmec area, often in the form of fine green celts; in a number of studies, archaeologist and epigrapher Karl Taube has shown that these were symbolic representations of ears of maize, the principal focus of Olmec religion. Some of the best jades are of a beautiful light blue color, and were apparently quarried in the mountains near Guatemala's Motagua River, a region where ancient tectonic plates had subducted to produce the conditions under which jade is formed.

All Olmec art, whether in jade, clay, or stone, is extraordinarily beautiful, and its religious iconography is highly complex. In fact, it is no exaggeration to say that the Olmec invented most of the major gods worshiped throughout time and space in Mesoamerica. Indeed, Olmec influence can be detected in many of the nascent civilizations of Mesoamerica, including, as we shall see, the Maya.

The big question is, what language or languages did the Olmec of San Lorenzo, La Venta, and other centers speak? Many scholars think that it was an ancestral form of Mixe-Zoquean, a linguistic family that includes a few tongues still spoken within the "Olmec heartland"; others have suggested that it might have been Mayan. We probably will never know, as we have no readable Olmec writing. The mystery remains.

THE MAYA PRECLASSIC: A GIANT STIRS

I have mentioned that Maya lowland culture during the apogee of the San Lorenzo Olmec was amazingly backward, and the Maya area proper may then have been only lightly populated. After about 1000 BC, this forested world began to change, possibly under the influence of La Venta to the west. To get at the earliest Maya constructions is no easy task, however, for the later Maya of the Late Preclassic and Classic periods built on the layer-cake principle. This entailed not the obliteration of old structures to build new ones, but the adding of buildings on top of older ones—the latter preserved to provide needed height as well as to honor the ancestors who had constructed those more ancient edifices.

In recent decades archaeologists working in the Petén of northern Guatemala and elsewhere in the lowland Maya area, have discovered huge, deeply buried earth and clay platforms dating to the Middle Preclassic (ca. 1000–400 BC); at the important site of Ceibal on the Río Pasión, these early temple builders had interred offerings of polished jade celts that may well have been made at La Venta.

From about 400 BC on, massive temple construction was found all over the lowlands, often on an impressive scale. These buildings and platforms were constructed of earth and limestone fragments, and usually faced with limestone blocks—remember that the entire peninsula is one vast limestone shelf. Over them a thick outer layer of white stucco was applied; frontal stairways were recessed and flanked by colossal stucco masks of gods, often painted. Since the manufacture of stucco entails the burning of limestone chunks with huge quantities of firewood, the result must have been major deforestation over wide areas and eventually an increase in erosion and the silting up of shallow waterholes and ponds. The consequences of this profligate use of forest resources will be apparent in later sections.

SAN BARTOLO

I have mentioned "gods," and it must be said here that the Maya religious system in its full complexity was already present in the Late Preclassic period (400 BC–AD 250). This became apparent in 2001, through one of those lucky chances that often result in great archaeological discoveries. On a hot day in the dry season of that year, at the small site of San Bartolo, in the far northeastern corner of Guatemala, William Saturno, then a researcher with Harvard's Peabody Museum, took refuge from the sun in a looter's tunnel that had penetrated the base of a ruined pyramid. What he found there, left untouched by the would-be thieves, was one of the greatest of all Mesoamerican murals, a virtual window into the supernatural world of the Late Preclassic Maya.

This masterpiece had originally been painted, around 100 BC, on the upper interior walls of a four-sided, flat-roofed building. Two of these walls had been demolished during an ancient rebuilding process, and two were still intact. Many fragments lay in the rubble, and are now being refitted in the project's laboratory. The north wall shows a zoomorphic Flower Mountain (see pages 126–27), complete with flowers and flitting oropendola birds; from its maw-like cave extends a feathered serpent, symbolizing the cloud-bearing breath of the mountain interior. Standing on the body of this snake we see the handsome young Maize God, his profile visage purely Olmec, along with his wife and other attendants, bearing in their hands the water and food that they have carried from this "mountain of sustenance."

The reconstructed west wall of the San Bartolo structure deals with mythic material that we know from the *Popol Vuh*, the sacred book of the K'iche' Maya, written down in Roman letters in the early colonial period. In it, a pair of Hero Twins (Hunahpu and Xbalanque) shoot with their blowguns a monstrous bird who arrogantly claimed to be the Sun, after this creature alights on a tree to eat its fruit. The mural depicts four Hunahpus, arrayed at the four cardinal points, each sacrificing blood from his own penis before one of these cosmic trees and the giant avian.

This is no ordinary bird, for he has a huge, pendant beak and quasi-human characteristics, and wears the headdress of the Maya supreme deity, known as Itzamnaaj. Mayanists have designated him as the Principal Bird Deity (or PBD for short), and it is his massive stucco mask that so often flanks stairways on Late Preclassic temples.

EL MIRADOR

On December 6, 1930, a Sikorsky amphibious biplane headed southeast from the Gulf of Mexico on an exploratory expedition mounted by the University Museum, Philadelphia. As it crossed the border from Mexico into northern Guatemala, it entered a heavily forested region known only to *chicleros*, tappers of the sap that would be converted into chewing gum. In the words of Percy Madeira, the expedition's director:

> The country was rising gently along our course to the east and we were flying at about 2000 feet, just under the cloud line. What looked like the cone of a volcano appeared on the skyline far, far ahead and a little to the south of our course, which was altered so that we headed for it. The elevation was so large and so distant that we feared it would prove to be a natural mound. . . . This big mound turned out to be the largest of a group of four artificial elevations, almost at the summit of a ridge. . . . Masonry was clearly seen in several places, and there is little doubt that this is the site of a really important new ruined city.

And so it was. This was the great, Late Preclassic city of El Mirador, and the "volcano" is now known to be the tallest pre-Columbian pyramid in the Western Hemisphere, and in bulk the most massive pyramid in the world.

Left: *Summit of the Danta structure, the largest pyramid of the Pre-Columbian New World. El Mirador, Late Preclassic, 300 BC–AD 100.*

Overleaf: *A jungle-shrouded plaza at El Mirador, Guatemala.*

A few years ago I had the good fortune to take a helicopter flight from Flores, the island capital of the Department of Petén in northern Guatemala, northwest to the great ancient city of El Mirador, just south of the Mexican border. We were traveling over virtually unbroken jungle, when in the distance could be seen the summits of two great structures rising above the 46-meter (150-foot) high forest canopy: the pilot told me that this was El Mirador itself. Yet beyond El Mirador, there were other structures on the distant horizon—these were ancient cities almost as large as the one we were flying toward. It reminded me of seeing the skyscrapers of Manhattan from the deck of the Triboro Bridge.

El Mirador lies in the Mirador Basin, a roughly triangular region covering a little over 2,070 square kilometers (800 square miles). During the Late Preclassic period, from about 300 BC to AD 150, this was the center of the Maya world, with eleven cities, five of which were true giants: El Mirador, Nakbé, Tintal, Xulnal, and Wakná. One finds extensive seasonal wetlands called *bajos* throughout this basin, and in many other places in the southern Maya lowlands. These are filled with water during the May-to-December rainy season, but as the dry season advances, they eventually dry up. As anyone who has lived or worked in the area knows, drinking water is exceptionally scarce for part of the year; one can die of thirst in the midst of the jungle. However, it appears that during the Late Preclassic, these wetlands were more like perennial, shallow lakes, in part fed by channels originating in the "built landscape" that was El Mirador. But that happy situation did not last forever, as we shall see.

El Mirador and the other 2,000-year-old cities of the area were linked to each other by enormous *sakbe'ob*, or "white roads"—great causeways built of crushed limestone; one reaching El Mirador from Tintal is 39 kilometers (24 miles) long. Similar causeways joined different temple complexes within El Mirador's 39 square kilometers (15 square miles) of pyramids and other structures.

The temples of El Mirador are basically huge, stepped pyramids of mixed earth and limestone rubble, faced with cut limestone blocks extracted from nearby quarries. One might have expected these great building stones to have been placed horizontally, but instead, the architect-overseers had them placed "head-on" into the mass of the substructure, providing great stability and strength but requiring at least three times more materials than otherwise. At the summits of these pyramids and platforms was one large temple building with two

An excavated temple-pyramid, El Mirador. Like other Late Preclassic structures in the city, this was built of massive limestone blocks and then covered with a thick coating of lime plaster.

smaller ones on either side of the upper platform. This "triadic" arrangement was found throughout the Mirador Basin and must reflect the triple nature of the unknown gods who were worshiped there. The larger of these temples seem to have had flat roofs supported by wooden beams, while the smaller ones had palm-thatched roofs. All of these structures were covered in thick layers of white stucco and painted with red hematite, colossal undertakings in their own right.

A good example of such a temple that has been fully excavated and restored is the relatively small Structure 34 of El Mirador. A four-tiered basal platform in the form of an inverted T is reached by the usual inset stairway; on it rests the usual triad of two subsidiary temples and the principal temple. The latter is fronted by another recessed stairway, which is flanked by two enormous stucco masks of a somewhat anthropomorphic PBD.

Consider now the Danta temple-pyramid, lying at the terminus of a long *sakbe*. This vast, complex structure is 72 meters (236 feet) tall, and is estimated to have a volume of 200,000 cubic meters (260,000 cubic yards), far outstripping Egypt's Great Pyramid in bulk. To raise such an architectural behemoth was a mind-boggling task: its facing consisted of limestone blocks oriented *inward*; the inhabitants lacked metal tools to shape these blocks and, as beasts of burden were unknown in ancient Mesoamerica, all materials had to be carried on human backs. Archaeologist Richard Hansen, the director of the Mirador Basin project, estimates that 15 million man-days were necessary to build the Danta pyramid alone, not to mention all the other triadic temples, platforms, and plazas within the city's confines.

This raises the thorny question of how many persons could have lived at that time in this huge city? Was the bulk of the labor force engaged in building activities from within El Mirador, or from the surrounding countryside? We should think of lowland Maya cities as consisting not of streets and avenues and city blocks like those of Chinese or Mesopotamian cities, but rather of low-density urbanism, with no street plans at all. Even so, given the huge size of the undertaking, the population of El Mirador and its suburbs could not have been much less than 100,000 persons, and probably a lot more.

Such a multitude of mouths to feed must have required the production of an agricultural surplus. There has been much speculation as to whether the margins of the *bajos* could have been used for maize agriculture, in addition to the *milpas* (shifting maize fields) in the surrounding hinterland, but there is little evidence to support this idea. Certainly these wetlands could have provided adequate drinking water for the city at its height.

How might have such a megalopolis been governed? Was the Mirador Basin under the sway of one dynasty? There is a curious scarcity of stone monuments in El Mirador and other neighboring cities that could have thrown light on this question. A very large number of fine, "codex-style" pottery vases were looted in modern times from small structures in Nakbé that date to a Late Classic re-occupation of the site. Of these, eleven list the names and accession dates of a series of nineteen kings belonging to the Kan ("Snake") Dynasty. Now the great city of Calakmul during the Classic period was ruled by the very same dynasty; as none of these names appears on Calakmul's own monuments, it is believed by scholars that the personages on the "dynasty vases" could have been the Preclassic lords of El Mirador. This is an intriguing idea that has yet to be confirmed.

All this amazing activity in the Mirador Basin during the Late Preclassic came to an abrupt end about AD 150. The entire area was completely abandoned, not to be reoccupied until six centuries later, during the Late Classic period. This was a cultural and demographic collapse matching the downfall that befell the lowland Maya in the eighth and ninth centuries AD. What brought it about? Richard Hansen has convincingly laid some of the blame on the demise of the *bajos* as a resource, almost certainly due to the massive deforestation, erosion, and silting-up brought about by the production of staggering amounts of the lime stucco that covered every building, platform, and pyramid. Add to this the agricultural debacle caused by climate change in the form of catastrophic drought.

These weakened city-states of the Mirador Basin, even huge capitals like Nakbé and El Mirador, seem to have been attacked by foreign armies, specifically by troops from the great military empire centered upon Teotihuacán, in central Mexico. The exterior of the great El Tigre pyramid was covered with dart points, many of them of green obsidian, which we know was obtained from highland Mexican mines controlled by Teotihuacán. Elsewhere in the Maya lowlands at this same time or a bit later, dated hieroglyphic records tell us of the eventual "arrival" of foreign kings from the west (that is, from Teotihuacán), invaders who overthrew the local dynasties to establish their own.

Two stucco friezes from a temple platform at El Mirador. Above, cormorants alternate with symbolic clouds amid an undulating band of water. Below, a pair of god impersonators swims or dives through water. Late Preclassic, 300 BC–AD 100.

RIVAL GIANTS of the CLASSIC PERIOD

 During the Classic period (AD 250–925), the Maya lowlands saw the rise of rival city-states of varying sizes and degrees of influence, in a social and political world like that of Classical Greece and Renaissance Italy, marked by wars, diplomatic relations, and exchange of high-ranking spouses between states. These polities were headed by powerful dynasties, some of which had their origin in the Preclassic period, and by hereditary rulers who claimed to be "divine kings." The major rivalry was between two giant city-states—Tikal and Calakmul—amid a complex political network of alliances and armed conflict that covered much of the southern Maya lowlands.

But the picture of these Maya lords operating in a kind of vacuum is far from simple, for it now appears that during the Early Classic (AD 250–600), the distant, highland Mexican state of Teotihuacán had massively intervened in Maya affairs, usurped the authority of native dynasties, and probably incorporated the entire Maya world—highland, lowland, and Pacific coast—into a huge, pan-Mesoamerican empire. This state of affairs ended when the great city of Teotihuacán was destroyed by unknown hands by the end of the sixth century AD.

*A spider monkey cavorts atop
a Tikal structure.*

TIKAL

On October 3, 1839, those pioneering explorers Stephens and Catherwood made their first Central American landfall in the port town of Belize, the capital of what was then the colony of British Honduras. Their immediate goal, the ruins of Copán, lay well to the southeast, and eventually they made their way there. If instead these two had headed west-southwest to the headwaters of the Belize River and proceeded inland from there, they would have discovered the mightiest Maya cities of all, and the true core area of Maya civilization. Tikal, for instance, lies only 153 kilometers (95 miles) in a straight line from Belize City. Yet in all of their great explorations in Maya country, they never penetrated the northern Petén of Guatemala or the southern part of Campeche and Quintana Roo.

The two eventually found themselves in the Guatemalan highlands, on their way to the ruins of Palenque. In the month of April 1840, in the town of Santa Cruz del Quiché, they made friends with a jolly Spanish priest who told them about what lay to the north of the Cuchumatanes *sierra* (mountain chain). He had been a curate at Cobán, a town in the hilly province of Alta Verapaz. According to him, about four leagues (16 miles) north of Cobán there was an ancient city:

deserted and desolate, and almost as perfect as when evacuated by its inhabitants. He had wandered through its silent streets and over its gigantic buildings, and its palace was as entire as that of Quiché when he first saw it. This within two hundred miles of Guatimala [Guatemala City], and in a district of country not yet disturbed by war; yet, with all our inquiries, we had heard nothing of it.

Opposite: *Temple I, Tikal, the funerary temple-pyramid of Jasaw Chan K'awiil I, dedicated in AD 734. Its soaring roof comb once bore a stucco portrait of the seated king.*

Overleaf: *The Great Plaza of Tikal is dominated by Temple I. On the left can be seen the North Acropolis, the burial place of Tikal's Early Classic rulers, fronted by a row of dynastic stelae. On the right is the Central Acropolis, the royal palace.*

It is suggestive that if we ignore the "four leagues north of Cobán" statement, and instead go 322 kilometers (200 miles) north of Guatemala City as the crow flies, we land in the middle of the Tikal archaeological park.

Of even more interest to our pair of explorers was a further assertion by the padre that:

four days on the road to Mexico, on the other side of the great sierra, was a living city, large and populous, occupied by Indians, precisely in the same state as before the discovery of America.

From the village of Chajul, he climbed to the topmost ridge of the sierra, at a height of ten or twelve thousand feet:

from which . . . he looked over an immense plain extending to Yucatan and the Gulf of Mexico, and saw at a great distance a large city spread out over a great space, and with turrets white and glittering in the sun. The traditionary account of the Indians of Chajul is that no white man has ever reached this city; that the inhabitants speak the Maya language, are aware that a race of strangers has conquered the whole country around, and murder any white man who attempts to enter their territory.

Stephens and Catherwood were understandably excited:

One look at that city was worth ten years of an every-day life. If he [the priest] is right, a place is left where Indians and an Indian city exist as Cortez and Alvarado found them; there are living men who can solve the mystery that hangs over the ruined cities of America; perhaps who can go to Copan and read the inscriptions on its monuments.

Alas, the dream of a still-inhabited Maya city in the Petén jungles was just that, a dream. But Stephens's paragraphs must have been read by the late Victorian novelist H. Rider Haggard, who made them the basis of one of the greatest adventure stories of all time, *Heart of the World* (1895).

Temple I, Tikal, seen through a door in the royal palace. The sapodilla wood lintel beams at the top are original. In the middle foreground is one of the very few ball courts in this immense city.

The towering temple-pyramids of Tikal are virtually iconic in the public consciousness of the Maya civilization. Their appearance in the first-released episode of the epic film series *Star Wars* was almost to be expected—to modern eyes, this is what a strange, jungle-shrouded civilization should look like.

First settled by Maya villagers in the Middle Preclassic, perhaps around 900 BC, by the end of the Late Preclassic Tikal had grown into an important center in the central Petén, but by no means on the scale of the mighty cities of the Mirador Basin. However, unlike those, it survived the end-of-the-Preclassic collapse. By the time of its apogee in the early eighth century, during the Late Classic, Tikal was indeed a very large city—although still smaller than El Mirador had been a millennium earlier. Like El Mirador—and all other Classic Maya cities—it had a low-density kind of settlement pattern, a dispersed form of urbanism with no arrangement of streets and avenues, no apartment blocks, nor any obvious municipal planning. Apart from what have been identified as royal palaces, the population—both noble and commoner—dwelt in pole-and-thatch structures placed on low platforms of earth and stone. What one finds is that the closer to the city's core, that is, to its concatenation of plazas, palaces, and ceremonial buildings, the larger the domestic structures. With this kind of settlement pattern, it is not always easy to define a city's limits. As Peter Harrison (one of Tikal's excavators) tells us, Tikal roughly covered 65 square kilometers (25 square miles), with over 3,000 known surface structures and a population variously estimated at between 100,000 and 200,000 souls.

As mentioned earlier, the Petén of northern Guatemala is not as well watered as one would expect for a monsoon region in the Central American tropics, and water for drinking and other domestic purposes could be in short supply during the dry season. The Tikal Maya accordingly excavated six reservoirs in the limestone bedrock and made sure that the runoff from the city's major architecture drained into them. Deep wells would have been impossible, as the water table here is several hundred feet below the surface.

What today's visitor to Tikal sees first is the Great Plaza at the center of the site; on its east and west sides, two great temple-pyramids, Temples I and II, face each other. On the north side is the North Acropolis, which could be more accurately described as a "necropolis," for this is where the early rulers of Tikal were entombed—the Maya equivalent of Egypt's Valley of the Kings. On its south is the massive, complex Central Acropolis, most probably the main royal

A pyramid in one of Tikal's Twin Temple groups, each consisting of two four-sided platforms fronted by stelae and altars. The stelae mark the end of k'atuns (20-year periods). This k'atun dates to AD 771.

palace during Tikal's later history. Leading out from the Great Plaza are three immense *sakbe'ob* (causeways, ceremonial roads), each of which leads to other soaring temple-pyramids. To the south of the west-leading causeway is the great Mundo Perdido, or "Lost World," plaza, with the most important buildings of Tikal's earliest history. A visitor to a Classic site like Tikal at its glory would have seen a city strikingly different from what today's tourists see; instead of white limestone blocks weathering to gray, our early pilgrim would have beheld an entire city and all its structures enrobed in thick, white stucco almost completely coated with a layer of red hematite pigment.

Also to be seen along the causeways, or at their termini, are five "Twin Temple" groups. Each complex consists of a pair of four-sided pyramids placed on the east and west of a platform, and strangely devoid of superstructures. On the north and south are two modest-sized temples. These complexes are known to have been erected to commemorate the completion of *k'atuns* (calendrical cycles measuring about twenty years).

To the modern visitor, Tikal indeed looks like a big place, and so it was in Maya terms. But viewed in the context of world civilization (or even compared with Teotihuacán), it was not all that gigantic. For example, take the medieval city of Angkor in Cambodia: very similar in its dispersed-urban settlement pattern, it is now known to have covered almost 1,000 square kilometers (about 400 square miles)—sixteen times the size of Tikal. And it is now apparent that the frontiers of Tikal, the largest Classic Maya city-state, were no more than a day's march from the center of its Great Plaza. As shall be seen, Tikal exerted long-distance control or at least influence over a wider area, but, as archaeologist Stephen Houston reminds us, this was no more extensive than the area covered by modern Ireland.

DYNASTIC HISTORY AT TIKAL

The long history of the ruling dynasty or dynasties of this great polity is richly documented by hieroglyphic texts, both carved on stone stelae and painted on pottery vessels. All great Maya lords took the title *Ajaw*, "King," and named themselves "holy king of such-and-such a polity." The real name of the Tikal polity was *not* Tikal (this may have been bestowed by unknown nineteenth-century visitors) but Mutul, expressed as a so-called Emblem Glyph in the form of a bound hank of hair.

A corbel-vaulted room in the Central Acropolis, Tikal's royal palace. All surfaces were once covered with thick lime plaster.

The 800-year-long story begins about AD 90, in the Late Preclassic, with a king known as Yax Ehb Xook (First Step Shark). He and his successors over the next three centuries were responsible for beginning the immense Lost World group, with its radial, four-sided pyramid, and it was they who started interring their dead predecessors in richly stocked tombs within the North Acropolis. This brings us to the initial decades of the Early Classic, by which time there began to be architectural and artistic influences from Teotihuacán. This trend was soon to reach an entirely new level. As Maya epigraphers Nikolai Grube and Simon Martin tell us, "Few, if any events had such a transforming effect on the Maya lowlands as the arrival at Tikal of a lord named Siyaj K'ak' (Fire Born) on 31 January 378." This person is known to have passed, five days earlier, through the city of El Perú, 79 kilometers (49 miles) west of Tikal. We have every reason to believe that he was a war leader from the powerful, militaristic Teotihuacán state in the highlands of Mexico, and that he swept into the central Petén at the head of his army, killing the last native Maya king of Tikal, Chak Tok Ich'aak (Great Burning Claw), and thereby overthrowing its dynasty. In short order, he installed in the slain king's place a new ruler named Yax Nuun Ayiin, the son of an exalted foreign personage named Spear-thrower Owl—quite possibly the supreme authority in distant Teotihuacán, perhaps even its emperor.

This was no isolated incident. Although many Mayanists persist in viewing the Teotihuacán presence throughout the Maya area during the Early Classic as mere cultural interchange between equals, I think it is inescapable to conclude that all of it—from the north coast of the Yucatán Peninsula and south to the Pacific coast—was part of a Teotihuacán Empire. To quote William of Occam's famous dictum, "neither more nor more complex causes are to be assumed than are necessary to account for the phenomena." In actuality, there is far more *archaeological* evidence for a "Pax Teotihuacana" in Mesoamerica than there is for the Aztec Empire—our knowledge of which rests largely on post-Conquest historical accounts. It should also be noted that the Aztec war machine never conquered the Maya, but the Teotihuacán military machine very definitely did.

What the Teotihuacanos brought with them was a "New Order," as Martin and Grube have called it. This included the cult of their war god, a jade-spangled serpent with the head of a deity later identified with the Aztec rain god, Tlaloc: goggle-eyed and topped by the sign for the year. This head would be worn as a mask or headdress

The Mundo Perdido, or "Lost World," temple-pyramid, a very early and complex structure built up by successive renovations extending from about 500 BC to AD 650. Giant stucco deity masks once flanked the central stairway.

by subsequent Maya rulers right through the ninth-century Collapse. Teotihuacán warriors fought with darts tipped with green obsidian and propelled by the *atlatl*, or "spear-thrower," a weapon far more effective at long range than the native Maya thrusting spear. All Mesoamericans practiced human sacrifice, but the Teotihuacanos seem to have done this on an unprecedented scale. Their Maya subjects were not exempt from this: recent excavations at the Pyramid of the Moon in Teotihuacán have uncovered a very special kind of offering, a group of what appears to be three sacrificed Maya kings, with all their jade finery.

Wherever they went, the Teotihuacanos introduced their own architectural style, based on the *talud-tablero*, a rectangular entablature placed atop a sloping batter. We find such structures at the highland site of Kaminaljuyú (on the western outskirts of modern Guatemala City), and at Petén sites, including Tikal. Every Maya city probably had a contingent of Teotihuacán troops; a recently discovered mural at Sufricaya shows them seated in military order with their weapons.

Yet, just as the Greeks who had been conquered by the Roman state eventually transformed the culture of their conquerors, so the new, foreign kings of the subjugated Maya city-states gradually became Mayanized. On a stela dedicated in AD 445, Siyaj Chan K'awiil, the son and heir of Yax Nuun Ayiin, is shown covered in purely Maya finery and symbols, but the double portrait of his father flanking the central figure depicts him as the central Mexican warrior that he in fact was. The North Acropolis continued to be the final resting place of these Maya-Mexican kings, their tombs richly stocked with pottery and other offerings of both Teotihuacán and native Maya manufacture.

For reasons that are not entirely clear, the first half of the sixth century marked a time of troubles for Tikal. Internal intrigues and confusion reigned, perhaps reflecting the destruction of that faraway exemplary city, Teotihuacán. These "Dark Ages" culminated in Tikal's defeat in AD 657 during a "star war"—a war set by a particular position of the planet Venus in the night sky against the background of the stars. The rival Calakmul state was the victor. After that event, no dated monuments were erected until AD 692. So weak was Tikal during these "Dark Ages" that one faction within Tikal's royal family broke away to form a new polity (Dos Pilas) 90 kilometers (54 miles) to the southwest, soon allying itself with Calakmul.

A plaza of the Central Acropolis, Tikal, with Temple I in the background.

Tikal's fortunes changed in AD 682, with the accession to power of its greatest king, Jasaw Chan K'awiil I. His supreme architectural monuments are Temples I and II, soaring structures that face each other on the east and west sides of the Great Plaza. Each rises up in nine tiers, with narrow, almost slot-like rooms on top; each is surmounted by a so-called roof comb, an elaborately stuccoed and painted construction that served as a kind of billboard advertising the king and his gods.

Temple II was dedicated to Jasaw's wife, but Temple I to the great man himself. One of the extraordinary wood lintels over its doorway proclaims his great victory over Calakmul in AD 695, when, bedecked as a Teotihuacán warrior, he captured and sacrificed a personage who was none other than Calakmul's mighty king Yich'aak K'ahk' (Fiery Claw). Jasaw had built this pyramid to house his own tomb, placed within it at its base and most likely reachable by a small tunnel to be closed in after his death and interment, which probably occurred in AD 733. This is the now-famous Burial 116, with a treasure trove of offerings, including a huge quantity of jade and pottery vessels to hold food and the chocolate drink. Also in his tomb was a set of bone tubes and strips delicately incised with mythological subjects, most notably a scene of the Maize God and other deities traveling in a canoe into the watery underworld.

To the Great Plaza's south lies the Central Acropolis, by now the principal royal residence, a vast limestone structure with multiple rooms. A glimpse of what life was like in these Late Classic palaces throughout the southern lowlands can be gained from scenes painted on cylindrical vessels used to contain the chocolate drink. Beneath swagged draperies, the enthroned ruler faces costumed courtiers, scribes, royal dwarfs, ambassadors bearing tribute, and others; wives and other women sometimes appear standing in front of the ruler or behind the thrones; and musicians blow on trumpets, play drums, and shake rattles. Among the grimmer scenes are the humiliation of captives and their sacrifice.

The immediate eighth-century successors to Jasaw maintained Tikal's architectural preeminence, even though its military power was slipping and other city-states were regaining their independence. The tallest pyramid-temple at Tikal, Temple IV, was raised by Yik'in Chan K'awiil, the twenty-seventh in the royal line, perhaps as his funerary monument (the base of this pyramid has not yet been explored). The truly amazing

A bound captive awaits his fate on a Late Classic altar at Tikal.

Temple VI sits at the terminus of the southeast causeway; discovered as late as 1957, the rear of its roof comb has a long inscription in monumentally sized hieroglyphs. The very latest of these soaring structures is Temple III, but by then (ca. AD 810), the city was already entering its irrevocable decline.

By the close of the ninth century, Tikal, like so many other cities of the southern lowlands, was well along the road to ruin and abandonment, with an ever-dwindling population living in its urban center.

CALAKMUL and the SNAKE KINGDOM

Only some 124 kilometers (75 miles) separate the center of Tikal from Calakmul, its great nemesis to the north and perpetual rival for dominance over the southern Maya lowlands. The name of this kingdom was Kan (Snake), and its snake-head Emblem Glyph is found wherever Calakmul's power extended, whether military, diplomatic, or uxorial.

The administrative state was at least as large as Tikal's, in fact, probably a lot larger. Its total extent is variously estimated as between 8,000 and 13,000 square kilometers (3,100 and 5,000 square miles), and the city itself held at least 50,000 souls. It was built on a raised limestone ridge close to a large *bajo* (wetland). As at Tikal and all other cities in the Maya heartland, ground water was always in short supply or at least precarious, so the population relied on an extensive system of water control, with eight roughly rectangular reservoirs, as well as ponds and connecting canals. Within the more or less urbanized core there are seven *sakbe'ob* (causeways), and a very long one connects Calakmul to El Mirador (and, by extension, to other very early cities in the Mirador Basin).

From an analysis of dynastic texts on a series of Late Classic "codex-style" vases originating at Nakbé, it is reasonable to think that the Snake polity originated during the Preclassic period in the Mirador Basin, with El Mirador as its capital, and that the Snake rulers, their families, and their people moved to Calakmul following the cultural and demographic collapse of the basin cities. There was a major Late Preclassic and Early

Calakmul's Structure II, a massive temple-pyramid rising 55 meters (180 feet), symbolizes the overwhelming power of this city-state. It was built in successive stages from Preclassic times through the Late Classic.

Classic building program at Calakmul, but unlike Tikal, Copán, and other Classic Maya polities, there is little or no trace of contact with, or domination by, Teotihuacán. Calakmul's long-standing enmity with Tikal may have its roots in its rulers' determination to distance themselves from Mexican foreigners. No Calakmul king is ever shown in Teotihuacán war trappings, but a word of caution here—the overwhelming majority of Calakmul stelae are highly eroded and thus illegible.

Calakmul, like Tikal, has been mapped in great detail, so that it is possible to compare its settlement type with that of Tikal and other Maya cities. The population was extremely dispersed, occupying small compounds consisting of two or three thatched houses with whitewashed walls of wattle and mud daub, raised on low platforms (known as "house mounds" to archaeologists). One looks in vain for streets or avenues of any kind. By comparison with cities like Tikal and Calakmul, the average American suburb, such as Levittown on Long Island, would seem densely urbanized.

There are two massive temple-pyramids in the city's center, Structures I and II. These bear little resemblance to the temple-pyramids at Tikal's heart. In fact, Structure II, with a present height of 55 meters (180 feet), looks very much like the Danta pyramid at El Mirador; the summit of Danta is said to be visible from Structure II on clear days. It rises up in two great stages over an earlier Late Preclassic temple with elaborate stucco reliefs on its upper façade. Its upper stage was built in Late Classic times to contain the burial (Tomb 4) of an extremely important individual. On the basis of a splendid polychrome offering plate bearing his name, archaeologist Ramón Carrasco believes him to be Calakmul's greatest king, Yich'aak K'ahk' (Fiery Claw), who ruled from AD 686 until his death in 695. Inside the tomb were the remains of eight sets of jaguar paws, along with jade and shell ornaments, and near the skeleton's chest was a spectacular mask covered with an extremely fine jade mosaic and bearing teeth of white shell inlaid with jade (when great Maya kings smiled, their front teeth glistened with apple green jade).

We have a problem of identification here, though. It will be remembered that in AD 695 Tikal's Jasaw Chan K'awiil claims to have captured and presumably sacrificed Fiery Claw. How, then, could Tomb 4 at Calakmul be Fiery Claw's final resting place? One can imagine that Jasaw was more likely to have cut off his antagonist's head and thrown

Stela 58, Calakmul, erected during the reign of Bolon K'awiil, the ninth ruler. It marks the completion of a Maya k'atun in AD 771.

the corpse to the dogs than to have reverently returned the remains to Calakmul, or to have forgone the execution and allowed him safe passage back home. In the face of this dilemma, it has been suggested that it was not Calakmul's supreme leader, but a *sajal* (subordinate war leader) who underwent decapitation. Who can tell?

Other buildings in Calakmul's monumental center include a type of complex that archaeologists know as an "E-Group." It features a small, east-oriented temple-pyramid that faces three small temples on a north–south platform; known elsewhere in southern lowland sites from the Late Preclassic, these groups have sightlines from the center of the pyramid toward the east, marking sunrise positions at the equinox and the solstices.

To the northwest of Structure II lies a large acropolis-cum-palace grouping, including a plaza with a modest-sized masonry ball court. To its northeast is another similar complex, but without a ball court. The entire ceremonial-administrative center is bordered to the north by a long, 6-meter (20-foot) high wall running from east to west. What could be the purpose of such a barrier? Lying just north of the wall is the Chiik Nahb complex, a roughly square enclosure 200 meters (656 feet) on a side, comprising 4 hectares (almost 10 acres) of relatively flat ground. Unlike Calakmul's more formal architecture, the whole complex has an informal, ad hoc look, with rows of low, north–south stone alignments defining what must have been market stalls.

This mercantile aspect is stunningly displayed in an extraordinary series of murals painted on a small, radial pyramid in the center of the southern half of the Chiik Nahb complex. Protected by the overburden of a layer structure, these brilliantly colored paintings, which probably date to the seventh century, show market merchants and their wares, each individual identified by an accompanying glyphic text. There are merchants vending salt, shelled maize, maize tamales, pottery vases, tobacco snuff, and the maize gruel called *ul* in Maya. One scene shows an upper-class lady in a see-through blue dress placing an olla filled with the *ul* drink on the head of her little servant girl. In the history of Maya archaeology, this great find is a unique view into the daily life of the Classic Maya.

Five stelae placed before a Calakmul temple-pyramid. Like so many of Calakmul's monuments, they are now unreadable because of erosion.

Such markets probably existed in all Classic Maya cities, including Tikal. Apart from the high hostilities and diplomatic machinations of the elite who headed these city-states, and apart from the daily lives of the farmers, there was an active overland commerce involving the entire Maya lowlands, and perhaps the highlands, too. Of course, beasts of burden and wheeled vehicles were lacking in ancient Mesoamerica, but humans could carry huge loads over very long distances. One section of the Chiik Nahb murals shows a trader with staff in hand, bringing to market his wares, which are borne with a carrying strap or tumpline supported by his forehead.

Let us recall the dream of Stephens and Catherwood, and of their friend the jolly curate, that there yet existed in their own day an inhabited Maya city somewhere in the Petén. If it had been real, and had they strolled in its market among traders and buyers, the Chiik Nahb murals give a brilliant idea of what they might have seen.

Late afternoon sun picks out stelae at the foot of the mighty Structure II, Calakmul.

BEYOND CALAKMUL

KOHUNLICH

Opposite: *View east of the Acropolis at Kohunlich, actually a residential sector of this small city.*

Below: *Late Classic buildings at Kohunlich. The Acropolis is at right.*

Within the past two decades several new sites have appeared that almost certainly would have lain under the sway of the mighty Snake dynasty, rulers of Calakmul. One of these is Kohunlich, a small site to the northeast of Calakmul, notable for an Early Classic temple-pyramid once buried beneath a later construction, with a beautifully preserved carved and painted stucco facing emphasizing large-eyed visages of the Maya sun god, K'inich Ajaw.

Opposite and right: *Two views of the giant, painted-stucco mask of K'inich Ajaw, the Maya sun god, at Kohunlich. The tendrils curling from either side of the mouth represent divine breath. Early Classic, ca.* AD *450.*

BALAMK'U

About 43 kilometers (27 miles) north of Calakmul lies a site now known as Balamk'u, where professional looters had penetrated a pyramid and come upon one end of an extraordinary stucco frieze that was later professionally excavated and revealed in all its glory. Dating to the Early Classic period (about AD 300–500), this powerful carving formed the upper part of a temple façade and measures 17 meters (56 feet) long and 4 meters (13 feet) high. It shows three different, monstrous, potbellied toads, each sitting above a gigantic mountain-mask; from the wide-open maws of these strange creatures emerges a seated, cross-legged ruler. What does such a weird tableau mean? We know that in Late Classic Maya art and writing, the open-jawed toad with upraised head is a glyph reading *siyaj*, "is born"; the import of the three elements of each carving probably is that such and such a ruler was "mountain born."

A Late Preclassic to Early Classic temple at Balamk'u.

Right (gatefold front):
Panoramic view of the unique Early Classic stucco frieze at Balamk'u. Flower Mountain masks support toads with gaping mouths, which in turn support seated rulers.

Overleaf (gatefold back):
Carved blocks forming the top step of a stairway of Structure 33, Yaxchilán (see pages 66–73). Watched by a pair of dwarves, the great Bird Jaguar IV prepares to receive a gigantic rubber ball containing the inverted and bound body of a rival king. Late Classic.

DZIBANCHÉ

Another site that fell under Snake dynasty control is Dzibanché, located150 kilometers (93 miles) northeast of Calakmul. Though its later temple-pyramids show some affinity with Terminal Classic Río Bec–style architecture (see pages 129–45), there is an Early Classic hieroglyphic staircase with reliefs showing crouching captives taken in a battle led by King Yuknoom Ch'aan of Calakmul toward the end of the fifth century.

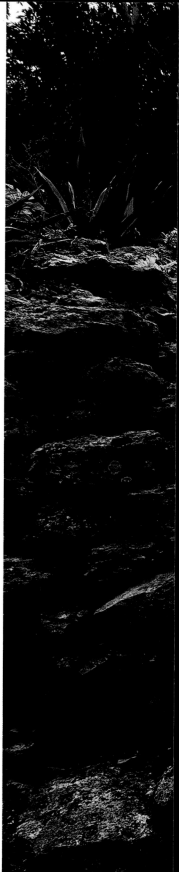

The corner of a possible residential building at Dzibanché, Quintana Roo.

Above: *Twisting roots of a strangler fig. The inner bark of this parasite was used by the Maya to produce paper for their folding-screen books.*

Opposite: *Temple II at Dzibanché, one of two temple-pyramids facing each other across a plaza.*

CITIES of the RIVER

One of the structures leading from the bank of the river to the higher temples of Yaxchilán.

THE USUMACINTA

"The River of Ruins," as the Usumacinta has been called in tourist literature, bears a name that is not Mayan, but Nahuatl—the language of the Aztecs and their highland Mexican allies (and adversaries). Before it was mispronounced by the Spaniards, it would have been *Ozomahtzintlan*, "Place of the Revered Spider Monkey(s)." How did a foreign name get attached to this, the seventh largest river in the world, and the largest in Mesoamerica? It is often overlooked that not only Spaniards took part in the Conquest—the conquistadores were often hugely outnumbered by willing Indian collaborationist troops, drawn mainly from highland, Nahuatl-speaking states like Tlaxcallan, who had long been enemies of the Aztec state. This is particularly true of the mixed Spanish-native armies that Alvarado took with him to subdue Guatemala. And that is why Nahuatl-derived place names instead of native Maya ones are found in Guatemala throughout its uplands and Pacific coast. So, when the Spaniards "discovered" this mighty river to the north of the sierra, they would have let their Mexican troops give it its name.

In the words of cartographer Ronald Canter, who has run (and documented) the entire course of the river, "The Usumacinta was one of the great water highways of the ancient world, but it was not an easy one." Today, it forms a significant frontier between Guatemala and southeast Mexico. It begins below the Classic Maya city of Altar de Sacrificios, which lies just above the confluence of its two great source rivers, the Pasión and the Salinas, and from there it flows in a generally northwest direction, finally emptying into the mangrove-lined coastal waterways bordering the Gulf of Mexico flatland. Apart from the tremendous

annual fluctuations in its volume and water level due to the alternation of wet and dry seasons, dugout canoes plying this mighty trade route faced many daunting challenges. In its upper and middle course, the Usumacinta passes through many Class 2–3 rapids, within limestone canyons whose walls can rise as high as 274–305 meters (900–1,000 feet) on either side, and powerful whirlpools can spin watercraft and smash them against rocks.

I have been on a float trip down these gorges, with pressure waves and all, and have wondered how Maya traders, without motorized launches or inflatable Zodiacs, could have negotiated this somewhat terrifying waterway. But negotiate it they did, for the great Classic kingdoms of Yaxchilán and Piedras Negras depended upon this commerce and fought with each other over its control. They were, in fact, river ports. Obviously, it was far easier to travel downstream than upstream, and truly skilled boatmen could easily handle rapids on the downriver trip. But upstream?

Though there are natural portages along the route, native dugouts made from a single log are incredibly heavy (as compared to the birch-bark canoes of North America), so this was seldom a practical solution. Since the late nineteenth century, Maya explorers have noted many limestone outcrops or natural pillars along the river that clearly served the Maya boatmen as bollards, with deep horizontal grooves caused by the friction of ropes that were used not only to moor boats but in many places to warp them up the rapids.

During the past few decades, conditions along this wonderful river have gone from bad to worse to truly frightening. The first cloud on the horizon was the Mexican government's intention to build a huge hydroelectric dam below Yaxchilán, which would have flooded that magnificent site along with countless others. An international outcry temporarily shelved this scheme, but hydroelectric dams, like the Hydra's heads, have a tendency to keep popping up, so the danger is still there. Then, during the Guatemalan Civil War (1960–96), control of this waterway on the Guatemalan side fluctuated between anti-government guerrillas and the Guatemalan army, resulting in massacres of local farmers. In the same period, lack of governmental control made it easy for looters to break up and remove Classic monuments for the antiquities market, Piedras Negras being the main target. While all this mayhem was going on, the Mexican side of the river was almost completely denuded of its rainforest cover as settlers poured in from the impoverished highlands of Chiapas, in part falling under the control of the Zapatista "Army of National Liberation." On the Guatemalan side of the river is the so-called Sierra de Lacandón National Park, but it is a "park" in name only, because it is now occupied by illegal settlers who have devastated its natural forest.

Right now the Usumacinta drainage is one of the world's most dangerous places, due in part to local banditry, but far more seriously to the sad fact that it has recently become a major conduit and battleground for the movement and control of narcotics on their way from Colombia to Mexico and ultimately to the United States. Add to this the constant flow of illegal migrants heading north from lower Central America, and the result is a truly lethal mixture. This has obviously not been good for Maya archaeology or for cultural tourism.

The upper half of a Late Classic stela at Yaxchilán; a woman passes a cord through a hole in her tongue to draw her own blood for the gods.

YAXCHILÁN

About a third of the way on its course to the Gulf Coast plain, the Usumacinta makes a bend in the shape of a great Greek omega, almost enclosing a hilly peninsula that can be reached by land only over a narrow neck. The founders of the Yaxchilán kingdom were wise to place their capital here, for it was easily defensible, and from its heights commanded all waterborne traffic like some baronetcy on a medieval European river. Only a few meters into the river from its south bank is a huge pile of stone that some speculate may have been a piling of an ancient but hypothetical suspension bridge crossing to the other side, but a more likely explanation is that it was a manned guard post for checking on river traffic. For four and a half centuries, Yaxchilán and its rival and enemy, the downstream city of Piedras Negras, were the generally uncontested rulers of much of the great river.

Neither of these two sites was ever seen by Stephens and Catherwood, even though they had the opportunity to hear of them during their April 1840 sojourn in Palenque, only 37 kilometers (23 miles) from the lower Usumacinta. The first serious investigation of Yaxchilán was undertaken almost simultaneously in 1882 by two noted explorers, the Englishman Alfred Maudslay and the Frenchman Claude-Joseph Désiré Charnay; before they met on the Usumacinta, neither had any idea that the other was on the track of this ancient city, but their meeting was a model of gentlemanly good sense. Désiré Charnay's Mesoamerican trip was bankrolled by his patron, the tobacco mogul Pierre Lorillard IV, and so he named the newly discovered site Lorillard City. Maudslay, on the other hand, called it Menché, after a local Maya family. Neither name stuck, however, so when the irascible Austrian archaeologist Teobert Maler arrived in 1897, he dubbed it Yaxchilán, after a local feeder stream below the site, and that is the name that finally won out.

Preceding pages: *One of the many mansard-roofed buildings of Yaxchilán.*

Left: *The back of Structure 33, the most splendid structure at Yaxchilán, with its lofty roof comb. It may have been built by Bird Jaguar IV, the city's most powerful king.*

Though we don't know the actual Classic Mayan place name for Yaxchilán, we do have two Emblem Glyphs for the dynasty that ruled it. One of these is the sky glyph, *chan*, with a cleft at the top; this probably is to be read either as *siyaj chan*, "sky-born," or as *pa' chan*, "split sky."

Today, Yaxchilán is one of the few truly safe places along the Usumacinta, and is easily reached by boat from a launch point upstream. There is something theatrical about the appearance of this ancient city. With most of its rainforest surroundings intact, it still resounds with the songs and calls of birds and the lionlike roars of a band of howler monkeys. Like a great stage set, its corbel-vaulted temples are dramatically placed on ever-ascending hills and ridges, reached from broad plazas via ceremonial staircases. The site boasts an enormous number of beautifully carved stone monuments; unlike those at Calakmul, they are fashioned from limestone of excellent quality, and thus most inscriptions are completely legible. There are as many as fifty-eight carved lintels over doorways, thirty-five freestanding stelae, and five hieroglyphic stairways, giving us a rich record of dynastic history and royal iconography.

Like the marble statuary of Classic Greece, all of these sculptures were once brightly painted and could be read and understood even more easily than they can today. To the modern eye, however, the lintels are a bit puzzling, as they were sculpted mainly on their underside—these important royal records can best be seen (and photographed) while lying on one's back!

Maudslay made papier-mâché molds of many of these monuments and brought back to the British Museum several of the finest and most deeply carved lintels; from these, his artist Annie Hunter made highly accurate drawings, which were later published in great detail. To this body of Yaxchilán hieroglyphic records Maler added his excellent photographic record, published in large format by Harvard's Peabody Museum of Archaeology and Ethnology. On the basis of these records, in 1963–64 the great Russian American epigrapher Tatiana Proskouriakoff succeeded in documenting the history of Yaxchilán's two greatest kings, Itzamnaaj Balam II (long called "Shield Jaguar" by archaeologists) and his son "Bird Jaguar."

Yaxchilán is modest in size (compared to Tikal or Calakmul, for example), but its full extent as a city is yet unknown; no comprehensive survey of its total settlement pattern has ever been made, and probably never will, unless the security situation can be stabilized. Its temples and palaces parallel the south bank of the river, and are placed along increasingly elevated natural ridges. The three loftiest temples (39, 40, and 41) lie on a ridge top 110 meters

Overleaf: *A small temple and an eroded stela at Yaxchilán.*

(361 feet) above the dry-season river level. All were once covered with lime plaster and painted red. Foreign dignitaries visiting the city during Bird Jaguar's reign in the eighth century—when Yaxchilán was in its most glorious period—would have left their huge dugout canoes tethered to a river bollard and proceeded with their entourage up to the main plaza. If they were to witness or participate in a ball game, they might have turned right, reaching one of the city's two masonry playing fields.

Directly across the plaza from this ball court, they might have paused to examine the three splendid doorway lintels of Temple 23, the so-called "Queen's Temple"—all celebrating important ceremonies involving Shield Jaguar's principal wife, Lady K'abal Xook. One depicts a ritual that took place in 681, in which the queen conjures a vision of her recently enthroned husband, who appears as a spear-wielding Teotihuacán warrior emerging from the jaws of a fantastic serpent—an homage to the great central Mexican city that had been in ruins for over a century. Another commemorates a nighttime bloodletting ceremony held eighteen years later: illuminated by a flaming torch held by Shield Jaguar, Lady K'abal Xook draws a thorn-bearing rope through a slit in her tongue, scattering blood into a basket. The third lintel depicts her handing her husband a war helmet in the form of a jaguar head.

Beneath the floors of two rooms in Temple 23, two tombs have been found. Under the central room, the burial of a woman was discovered, accompanied by nineteen jaguar claws arranged in three groups, nine carved-bone bloodletters, and eighty-one needles, all gathered into a single bundle. Six of the bloodletters bear Lady K'abal Xook's name, so this is surely her final resting place. Although neither this nor the other tomb found in the structure have yet been published in sufficient detail, it is likely that the buried woman is the great queen herself, who died in 749.

Shield Jaguar was the most long-lived Maya ruler known to us, dying in his nineties in June AD 742. Bird Jaguar was Shield Jaguar's son by a lesser wife; after a decade-long interregnum, he finally succeeded to the Yaxchilán throne. During his reign (AD 752–68), he remodeled the city and built many new structures to celebrate himself and his family. Simon Martin and Nikolai Grube call him "the warrior king," and there is no doubt that he deserved the epithet that follows his name in the inscriptions: "he of the twenty captives." If our visitors ascended the stairway leading southeast from the main plaza, they would have reached the city's most splendid building, Structure 33, with its corbeled superstructure surmounted by a

towering roof comb that once bore a stucco sculpture of the enthroned Bird Jaguar. Within its central room is a stone statue of the king. Bird Jaguar's broken-off head sits to one side of the seated torso; according to local Maya tradition, the world will come to an end if anyone has the temerity to place the head back on the torso!

The upper steps in front of the structure are of extreme interest for their reliefs of the royal father and son, and the grandfather, playing the ball game against a staircase seen in profile (see gatefold back between pages 56 and 57); the large and unlikely ball seems to contain a bound captive, probably symbolizing the custom in Classic Maya cities of forcing defeated enemies to play a match that they had no chance of winning, for which they had to suffer the consequences (we shall see this reflected later in the Great Ball Court of Chichén Itzá; see pages 203–4).

And finally, our visitors would mount to the highest structures of all, Temples 40 and 41, which celebrate events in Bird Jaguar's life. Most of our hero's victories resulted in the capture of important individuals from the lands lying between Yaxchilán and Piedras Negras, and under his rule the city retained control of centers like Bonampak and Lacanjá in the sierra country to the southeast of the river. But after his death in AD 768, the Yaxchilán polity began to wane, in spite of the fact that its last known ruler seems to have defeated and captured the last ruler of Piedras Negras. And not long after the ninth century began, Yaxchilán winked out.

The now-fallen Stela 11 at Yaxchilán. Bird Jaguar IV (on the right) faces his father, Shield Jaguar. AD 752.

BONAMPAK

In my estimation, the three most spectacular discoveries in the history of Maya archaeology—discoveries on a par with King Tutankhamun's tomb or the Terra-Cotta Warriors of Xi'an—are 1) Pakal's tomb in the Temple of the Inscriptions in Palenque, 2) the Late Preclassic wall paintings of San Bartolo, and 3) the magnificent Late Classic murals of Bonampak. The site of Bonampak lies only 20 kilometers (12 miles) southwest of Yaxchilán, in the drainage of the much smaller Lacanjá River, a branch of the Usumacinta.

Bonampak was unknown to the outside world until February 1946, when two young American adventurers were taken there by Lacandón Maya, but they failed to find the building with the murals for which the site is world famous. In May of that year, the Californian photographer Giles Healey, on commission from the United Fruit Company to make a film about the Maya, was taken by the Lacandón into Structure 1 ("The Building of the Paintings") and saw that all three of its rooms were covered from floor level to their corbel vaults with the most spectacular murals ever discovered in the New World. He soon was able to telegraph the Carnegie Institution of Washington, which posthaste mounted an expedition that

included the talented Guatemalan artist Antonio Tejeda, who copied these polychrome paintings at one-quarter scale.

What to call it? The local Lacandón had no particular name for these ruins. Undaunted, the famed Carnegie archaeologist Sylvanus Morley (following a quick look at a Maya dictionary) dubbed the site *Bonampak*, or "painted walls." Unfortunately, in Yucatec Maya this word really means "dyed walls," but the name has stuck in both the scholarly and popular press. There are at least two Bonampak Hotels in Mexico, as well as a Bonampak rum!

The site is relatively small, and lies on the side of a natural hill. The epigrapher David Stuart notes that it is oriented 30 degrees east of north; a line drawn along its main axis is aimed directly at Yaxchilán, probably a significant fact, as that city exerted a degree of political control over Bonampak. Its history as a small state began at least by the Early Classic, but it was not always propitious; during the fifth century a Yaxchilán king captured the lord of Bonampak, and early in the sixth century a Bonampak noble was taken by another Yaxchilán *ajaw*. However, a far more successful *ajaw*, Chan Muwaan (Sky Screech Owl) reigned during the city's glory days; it was he who was responsible for the amazing murals, as well as for three remarkably well-carved stelae depicting himself, his principal wife, and his mother, and for the finely sculpted lintels over the doorways of the buildings on the acropolis (some of which retain their polychrome overpainting). Powerful though he was, Chan Muwaan was still a suzerain and close ally of the Yaxchilán king Shield Jaguar III, the son of the mighty Bird Jaguar IV.

When Healey first saw the murals in the three rooms of Structure 1, they were covered by a very thin layer of calcium carbonate that had leached out from the upper part of the building over the ages. This layer had actually protected and preserved the paintings exactly as the Maya artists had left them over a millennium before. To photograph and copy them, the Carnegie group doused the wall surfaces with kerosene, a procedure that did little or no damage to the originals (kerosene evaporates in time). The real deterioration began when succeeding official Mexican expeditions to Bonampak cut down the trees growing atop the structure and replaced them with a galvanized tin roof, so that the walls were hot by day and cold by night. Subsequent interventions over the years by well-meaning conservators and restorers have been disastrous to these masterpieces, including the use

Preceding pages: Bonampak, view looking south from the front plaza. The building with the famous murals is on the far right.

Opposite: An orchestra of singers shaking rattles, a drummer, and musicians beating turtle shells accompanies a group of mummers (offstage, left). Bonampak, Late Classic, ca. AD 800.

Overleaf: Visiting dignitaries wearing long white capes attend a ritual in honor of Bonampak's youthful princes.

of silicone injections, filling in cracks with cement, and over-harsh cleaning. They are now but wan shadows of their former selves.

But all is not lost. Beginning in 1999, a research team led by Mary Miller of Yale University has been using multiband imaging (including infrared) to accurately reconstruct exactly what these murals looked like at the time they were painted. This has enabled artists Heather Hurst and Leonard Ashby to make half-scale reproductions of all three rooms. Miller's team includes epigrapher/ archaeologists Stephen Houston and Karl Taube, who were able to properly decipher the ancient texts in the paintings, including personal names, for the first time.

The early Maya artists were extremely sophisticated in the use of color, as Diana Magaloni of the National Autonomous University of Mexico has determined through chemical analysis. They used a wide color palette, often mixing pigments to produce different effects. Some of these pigments had to be imported over great distances, such as the mineral azurite, used for some shades of blue, which comes from the highlands of central Mexico. As she has discovered, there were several artists involved who worked *al seco*, that is, on dry plaster walls, mixing their colors with some kind of vegetal binder. These painters were masters at producing the illusion of three-dimensionality, not by perspective but by a kind of chiaroscuro, subtly backlighting their human figures (a technique also known to Late Classic vase painters).

The program of Room 1 centers on the presentation of a little daughter to the enthroned king Chan Muwaan on December 4, 790. To the right of the throne is a large sack of 40,000 cacao (chocolate) beans, brought as tribute. In attendance are visiting nobles arrayed in long, white capes. At the base of the room is an extended panel centering on high-ranking youths being adorned for a dance by servants with quetzal-feather backracks (large decorative structures

attached to the dancers' backs), to a musical accompaniment consisting of trumpeters, drummers, and singers shaking rattles. To the far left, a group of mummers masked as wind, rain, and sea creatures performs.

Room 2 is devoted to a huge battle in the forest and its aftermath. The Bonampak warriors are led by Chan Muwaan himself. The enemy combatants are speared and taken captive. The final scene takes place on a terraced platform, where Chan Muwaan's prisoners are arraigned and tortured by having their fingers crushed; a severed head rests on a bed of leaves. Above, watching all this, is the king, surrounded by his courtiers, his white-robed mother, and his principal wife, a woman from Yaxchilán.

Finally, in Room 3, in culmination of all this, magnificently garbed young nobles perform a whirling victory dance after sacrificing blood from their own members; below them, attendants drag a sacrificed prisoner down the steps. The blood theme is extended at one end of the room, where royal females draw their own blood from their tongues. After deciphering all the painted texts in the three rooms, Stephen Houston has concluded that this building was a kind of "Young Men's House," where the princes pictured in Rooms 1 and 3 were instructed in statecraft and military matters.

Needless to say, the discovery of Bonampak has been a catalyst in changing our views about the nature of Maya civilization. Before it, most authorities, such as Eric Thompson and Sylvanus Morley, had claimed that the Classic Maya were organized as a kind of peaceful theocracy in which the leaders were pacifist priests devoted to astronomy, mathematics, and the doings of the gods, not unlike the fictional Shangri-La—the Himalayan valley dreamed up by the novelist James Hilton. Given the vivid battle scene of Bonampak and its bloody aftermath, this view became untenable, although Thompson in his commentary on the paintings still downplayed the violent aspects of the pictorial drama created by these ancient artists.

Glorious wall paintings like those of Bonampak almost certainly existed throughout the Usumacinta drainage, but only tiny fragments have escaped erosion and disappearance, for instance in some rooms at sites like Yaxchilán and Pasadita. We can only be thankful for the lucky accident that preserved those three rooms in Bonampak's Structure 1. These murals may never have been completely finished; for instance, some of the spaces left for captions are completely blank. By AD 800, Bonampak was swiftly headed for the kind of oblivion that finished off all Maya cities of the southern and central lowlands.

Preceding pages, left:
On this finely carved stela, the Bonampak king Chan Muwaan (the commissioner of the murals), is flanked by two women, one of them his principal wife.

Preceding pages, right:
Lintel 4, Bonampak. The ruler holds a symbol of office, a bicephalic snake; from its mouth emerges K'awiil, the god of the royal house.

On Lintel 1 at Bonampak, Chan Muwaan spears a fallen enemy on June 6, AD 787.

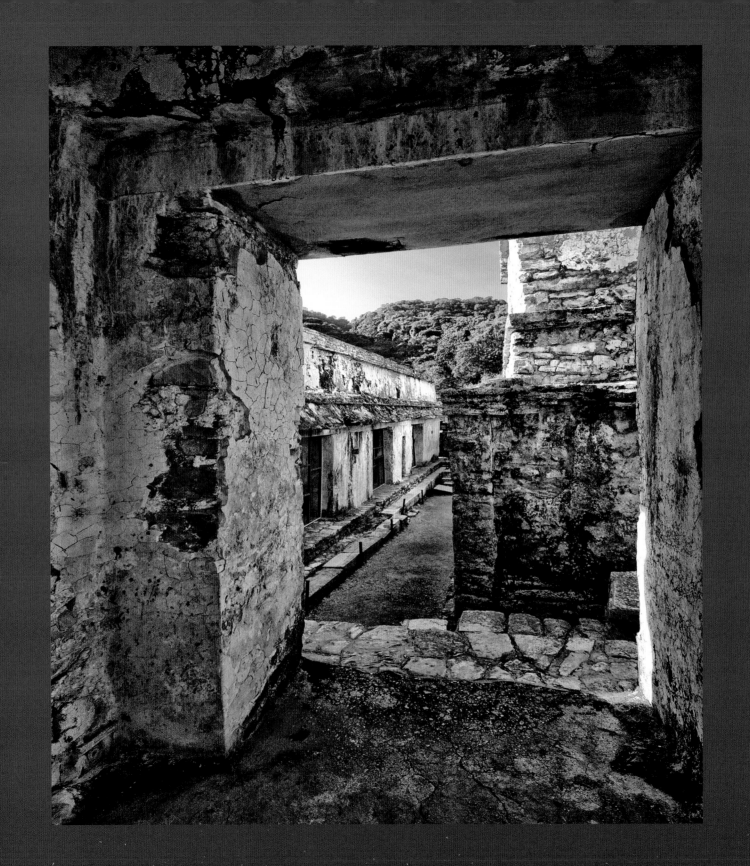

CITIES of the WEST

PALENQUE

We Mayanists are only human—like almost everyone who has had the chance to travel in Maya country, we each have our favorite site. For me and for many of my colleagues, it is Palenque. Situated on the northern edge of the Sierra de Chiapas, and still surrounded by tropical rain forest, it looks out over the vast Gulf Coast plain. Its architecture is airy and roomy, rather than solid and massive, its baroque stuccowork is both delicate and powerful, and its bas-relief panels (all carried out on lithographic-quality limestone) are incomparable. Add to this what is certainly the most complete hieroglyphic history yet known for any Maya city, a record that places its ruling dynasty within a far grander cosmic history, and one has to conclude that Palenque is unique.

Far from being a "lost city," Palenque has been known to the outside world intermittently since 1567, when the Spanish friar Pedro Lorenzo de la Nada learned about it from the local Chol Maya. By the late eighteenth century, these ruins had piqued the interest of the Spanish crown. In 1786 Charles III of Spain—that most enlightened of Bourbon kings— ordered a complete investigation, which was competently carried out by a talented military officer named Antonio del Río; it proved to be the very first research project on an ancient American site.

Published in translation in London in 1822, with plates prepared by the eccentric artist and explorer "Baron" Frédéric de Waldeck, the del Río report came to the attention of Stephens and Catherwood. And so it was that the two explorers arrived at the ruins in May 1840. Journeying there on muleback from the nearby, and decidedly miserable, village of Palenque (a Spanish word meaning "palisade"), they ascended a series of terraces to confront the ancient city for the first time:

View from inside the Palace at Palenque.

Continuing on this terrace, we stopped at the foot of a second, when our Indians cried out "el Palacio," "the palace," and through openings in the trees we saw the front of a large building richly ornamented with stuccoed figures on the pilasters, curious and elegant; trees growing close against it, and their branches entering the doors; in style and effect unique, extraordinary, and most mournfully beautiful.

Their wonder at the architectural and artistic beauty of the Classic city was echoed by most subsequent visitors, including archaeologists, but not by all. Here is what British author Graham Greene wrote about that same "el Palacio" almost a century later in *Another Mexico*:

. . . in the clearing itself there is nothing but a few Indian huts, scrub and stone and great mounds of rubble crowned with low one-story ruins of grey rock, so age-worn they have a lichenous shape and look more vegetable than mineral. And no shade anywhere until you've climbed the steep slopes and bent inside the dark little rooms like lavatories where a few stalactites have formed and on some of the stones are a few faint scratches which they call hieroglyphics.

Dyspeptic comments, to be sure, but then Greene didn't like *anything* about Mexico!

Let us return to Stephens and Catherwood. Their thirty-five-day stay among the ruins, and Catherwood's meticulous documentation of Palenque's extraordinarily complex architecture and bas-reliefs, took place under the most horrendous conditions. The rainy season began in earnest that month, with driving rain and falling tree branches. They were low on food, which had to be brought in over the eight-mile trail from the nearest village, and the food was poor at best. The mosquitoes, chiggers, and other biting insects plagued the explorers, especially Catherwood. At one point, says Stephens, "Mr. Catherwood's appearance

---

The Temple of the Inscriptions, completed in AD 692, is the funerary temple-pyramid of Pakal, Palenque's greatest king. His resplendent tomb lies at ground level, deep within the base of the pyramid.

startled me. He was wan and gaunt; lame, like me, from the bites of insects; his face was swollen and his left arm hung with rheumatism, as if paralyzed."

As usual, Stephens was able to draw absolutely correct conclusions about this ancient city: "The hieroglyphs are the same as we found at Copán and Quiriguá. The intermediate country is now occupied by races of Indians speaking many different languages and entirely unintelligible to each other, but there is room for belief that the whole of this country was once occupied by the same race, speaking the same language, or at least having the same written characters."

Serious archaeological excavations began in the 1940s by Mexico's National Institute of Anthropology and History (INAH), and continue to this day, revealing ancient splendors that prejudiced tourists like Greene had no idea existed.

The ancient Maya called the city Lakamhá, "Great Waters," from the many streams that course down from the heights behind and through the city onto the plain, in some places forming lovely pools. In 1955, when I first visited Palenque along with my wife, Sophie, one was still allowed to swim in the so-called Baño de la Reina (Queen's Pool), where tiny minnows nibbled ticks off one's skin. I remember a later visit with our small children, watching an iridescent hummingbird hovering over the lip of a cascade located above the pool, caught in a beam of golden sunlight. Palenque is indeed a magic place.

It was probably this abundant network of permanent streams that drew settlers here in the first place, for water in the Maya lowlands is usually a scarce resource, especially during the long dry season. The city has now been mapped in great detail by archaeologist Edwin Barnhardt, and it has been revealed as the most densely inhabited of all the Maya capitals. During Palenque's apogee, around 7,000 people could have lived within the rather small area of 2.2 square kilometers (0.8 square miles); in contrast to the widely dispersed settlement pattern of far larger cities like Tikal and Calakmul, this was cheek-by-jowl existence.

The ceremonial, religious, and political zone of the city lay in the eastern half; the bulk of the population lived in the western half. In their masterly book on Palenque, David and George Stuart suggest that the elite occupied dwellings on the lowest terrace, facing out over the plain, that is, commanding the best views. It is believed that almost all civic residences were fitted with thatched roofs, rather than masonry vaults.

MYTH AND HISTORY

In examining the long story of the dynasty that reigned in Palenque, we must disentangle mythological beginnings from the most likely historical facts. In their own inscriptions, the city's rulers traced their descent from sacred ancestors, and even from gods who were said to have been born in the fourth millennium BC, before the present Maya Great Cycle began. In actuality, archaeology tells us that though this extremely favorable location with its abundant waters probably had a small population during the Late Preclassic era, it is not until the fifth century AD that a real urban settlement with an actual ruling house can be identified.

The first attestable king called himself K'uk' Balam (Quetzal Jaguar), a royal name that was to pop up again with the second-to-last of Palenque's rulers, not long before the city's irreversible decline. At this time, during the Early Classic, Palenque may have been subject to the same kind of foreign military pressure as Tikal and other Maya capitals, as a stucco relief panel depicting the goggle-eyed Teotihuacán war god testifies.

Almost all of the glory of the Palenque that one sees today is the work of its three greatest rulers, who flourished during the Late Classic period. These men, and their successors, prefaced their names with the prestigious title *K'inich*, meaning "Sun-eyed," self-identifying with the mighty Sun God. They are:

> Janaab Pakal (Maize-flower War-shield), known today as Pakal or Pakal
>   the Great.He reigned from AD 615 to 683.
> His son Kan Bahlam (Snake Jaguar), AD 684–702.
> Pakal's grandson Ahkal Mo' Nahb (Turtle Macaw Sea), AD 721–ca. 736.

PAKAL THE GREAT:
ACHIEVEMENT AND LEGACY

Pakal was extraordinarily long-lived for a man of his time, acceding to power in AD 615 at the tender age of twelve, and dying sixty-eight years later, in his eighty-first year. The first king to use the solar title of K'inich, during his long reign Pakal transformed Palenque into both a military and a cultural power within the lowland Maya realm. As the Stuarts say, Pakal's achievements brought about "a true renaissance in the history of the city." As Pericles was to ancient Athens, Pakal was to Palenque.

One of his major projects, carried out in middle age, was initiating the first building stages of the so-called "Palace" (the *el Palacio* of Stephens and Catherwood and numerous other early visitors). This large, highly complex structure comprises several superimposed basal platforms, on which are placed one-story vaulted buildings arranged around inner courtyards. In spite of its popular name, there is no proof that anyone, including the royal family, ever actually lived in the Palace. Rather, it was surely dedicated to royal ceremonies and rituals.

Pakal commanded the very best architects in all of the Maya area, and the spaciousness and airiness of the Palace structures bear this out. Each "House" is built on the principle of the corbel arch, with two parallel corridors separated by a common wall, over which was placed a light, latticed roof comb. But instead of the huge bulk of the upper structure, as seen at other Maya sites, the architects opted for a mansard roof, niches, and the piercing of walls, which cut down weight and made possible inner spaces much wider than the slot-like ones in the temples of Tikal and other more central sites. Everywhere in the Palace and in all other temples in the site—especially on the outer surfaces of the piers between doorways—were stucco reliefs of the utmost elegance and delicacy. The artist and explorer Merle Greene Robertson, in her great survey of Palenque sculpture, determined that those who were responsible for the application of a final coat of color to reliefs (and all were so painted), used red and yellow for the bodies of humans, and blue for gods and glyphs.

Punctuating the outer edges of building cornices here and in other major structures of the city are pairs of holes drilled to support hanging textiles. Given the hot, humid climate, none of these hangings has survived the centuries, but they must have presented a splendid appearance during ceremonial occasions. Painted vases from other Maya sites often depict court scenes taking place below swagged curtains, and the gorgeous

Top part of a stucco figure on a pilaster of the Palace at Palenque. This individual holds a staff topped with the profile head of K'awiil, patron of the royal lineage.

Preceding pages: *Panoramic view of the Palace complex, Palenque. It was built and used by a succession of Palenque kings during the Late Classic period.*

Left: *Painted stucco panel from Temple XIX, Palenque. Possibly representing a brother of the ruler Ahkal Mo' Nahb, it was found in a multitude of small fragments, and is a masterpiece of modern restoration.*

costumes of the figures in the Bonampak murals indicate that the Maya were masters of the textile art.

The very first structure that Pakal built in the Palace was House E, which contained his own throne room. Against its far wall is an oval tablet depicting the king being offered a jade-spangled headdress by his mother at the time of his accession; the actual throne was once below this, but early explorers, including del Río, carted it away in various pieces.

The Baak (Bone) polity of Palenque was just as bellicose as the dynasties of other Maya city-states and was involved in frequent battles, especially with Toniná and the more distant but far mightier Calakmul. It would seem that the Palace's courtyards were favorite locales for the processing of elite prisoners of war, a treatment that involved humiliation, torture, and eventual decapitation. In the East Court, for instance, there are ludicrous relief caricatures of nine captives who give the sign of submission (left hand raised to the opposite shoulder), and one has his loincloth pulled aside to display his grotesquely enormous genitals.

A unique feature of the Palace is the four-story tower in its midst, a structure added in a later reign. Its purpose is unknown; a large Venus glyph painted on its interior has led some to think it was some kind of observatory, but there is no way to prove this.

Pakal's final achievement was the creation of the towering Temple of the Inscriptions, his funerary temple-pyramid, just southeast of the Palace. Taking advantage of the natural hill against which it was built, it rises in nine superimposed tiers to support a mansard-roofed building with two long, parallel rooms; regularly spaced along the façade are six pilasters adorned with stucco figures, a few holding in their arms an infantile form of the snake-footed K'awiil, one of the ancestral gods of the royal line. Set into the back walls of the two rooms are three panels of one of the longest inscriptions ever carved by the Maya, detailing ritual events in the life of Pakal the Great, probably put in place before the final dedication of the temple by Kan Bahlam in July 690.

A vaulted, secret passage descends from the floor of the front room into the body of the pyramid in two stages to reach the now world-famous tomb of the king, first opened in 1952 by Mexican archaeologist Alberto Ruz L'Huillier. Inside a huge stone sarcophagus he discovered Pakal's mortal remains, bedecked in the jade necklaces, ear flares, plaques, and finger rings that he had worn in life; a wood mask covered with jade mosaic had been placed over his face, identifying him with the young Maize God. Carved on the sides of

this enormous coffin were the figures of his immediate ancestors, emerging from the earth along with various fruit trees.

Following Pakal's entombment, a massive oblong slab was placed over the sarcophagus, depicting him as the resurrected young Maize God, about to ascend to the heavens via a world tree. Then the chamber was sealed, and the entire passageway filled with rubble, leaving a stone-lined conduit on one side of the stairway to conduct Pakal's soul to the upper world.

KAN BAHLAM AND THE PALENQUE TRIAD

Just to the east of the Temple of the Inscriptions lies the Cross Group, three temples dedicated in 692, during the reign of Pakal's son Kan Bahlam. In many respects, they represent the acme of Classic Maya art and architecture, and the pinnacle of Maya ideas about the relation between the ancestral gods and the divine kings who ruled this city-state.

The largest and most important of these structures is the Temple of the Cross, sitting on six superimposed platforms. Although part of its front collapsed long ago, one can still see a kind of inner shrine within, on the rear wall of which was placed a huge relief carving depicting a cruciform world tree (the same as the one on Pakal's sarcophagus) surmounted by the avian form of the Creator God, Itzamnaaj. On one side of the world tree is a small figure standing on the glyph for *wits*, "mountain," and on the other a taller figure holding out a small statue of the so-called Jester God, the symbol of kingship. We now know that these two figures are Kan Bahlam as a six-year-old boy and as the king at the time of his accession in AD 684.

Ever since it was drawn in detail by Catherwood and photographed by Maudslay and others, the very long text carved on either side of this scene has intrigued would-be decipherers. We now know that it begins with the birth of the Maize God in 3121 BC, seven years before the end of the last Great Cycle and the beginning of our own; it was he who was responsible for the creation of three other gods known to us as the Palenque

View from the Temple of the Cross, Palenque. On the left is the Temple of the Sun, built during the reign of Kan Bahlam. Seventh century AD.

Triad, the tutelary divinities of the royal house. The Temple of the Cross was dedicated to the worship of the first of these, a deity connected to water and rain.

The second shrine, the far smaller Temple of the Foliated Cross, has a similar inner sanctum, the tablet of which shows the same two versions of Kan Bahlam facing a huge maize plant as a world tree, and is clearly devoted to the infant form of the god K'awiil as the patron of abundance. Looking west across the plaza is the Temple of the Sun, in the opinion of many (including me), one of the most perfect buildings ever created by the Maya; it also has an inner shrine, in this case representing the visage of the Sun God as a war shield, with crossed spears. This trio of temples devoted respectively to rain or water, maize agriculture, and war suggests that the triadic layout of temples in great cities of the Late Preclassic, such as El Mirador, might have had a similar meaning.

Following Kan Bahlam's death in AD 702, he was succeeded by a brother who had the misfortune of being taken captive nine years later during a disastrous war with Toniná. Curiously, he was eventually released and allowed to live out his remaining years in Palenque. In AD 722 Ahkal Mo' Nahb was enthroned, and it was this ruler, a nephew of Kan Bahlam, who was responsible for a cluster of temples to the south of the Cross Group. In the past two decades excavations by INAH archaeologists have brought to light some of the most magnificent relief carvings ever produced by Classic artists, celebrating not only the patron-king but also his court and his all-important kinship with Pakal the Great.

Three more "Sun-eyed" kings succeeded, but not long after AD 800, Palenque (like Bonampak, Yaxchilán, and most of the city-states of the Petén) went into steep decline, ending in the extinction of the Baak dynasty and this beautiful city's abandonment to the encroaching tropical forest.

Two clay objects from Palenque depicting the Jaguar God of the Underworld, the night sun on its passage beneath the earth. On the left is a large figurine; on the right, a tall incense burner.

TONINÁ

Located some 64.5 kilometers (40 miles) due south of Palenque, Toniná occupies one of a series of parallel limestone ridges that extend from northwest to southeast in the rugged, hilly country of upland Chiapas. These ridges are separated by rivers that form part of the headwaters system of the Usumacinta; given this terrain, the actual overland distance between these two mutually hostile kingdoms was far greater than it seems on the map.

The ruins of Toniná have been known since the seventeenth century and visited by many later travelers. Stephens and Catherwood, while on their way to Palenque, stopped there only long enough for Catherwood to draw a partially preserved stucco relief on one of the buildings, which clearly represents one of the wings of the Principal Bird Deity (PBD). The first serious investigations began in the 1920s, with the explorations of Danish archaeologist Frans Blom and American writer Oliver La Farge. A French team excavated the site in the 1970s, and during the past two decades an INAH program under Mexican archaeologist Juan Yadeun has resulted in spectacular discoveries.

The ancient name of the Toniná state and the dynasty that ran it was Po (or Popo'); its kings were as militaristic as any in Maya history, in an almost constant state of war with enemies near and far, particularly Palenque. Situated on a limestone ridge at an altitude of 800–900 meters (2,600–3,000 feet), Toniná is the only highland Maya site with a lowland culture. Crowning this ridge is an enormous and lofty Acropolis, perched atop seven great terraces and facing

The enormous Acropolis of Toniná evokes the formidable power of this kingdom in the Chiapas foothills.

Above and right: *One of the lower stages leading up to the Acropolis summit, Toniná (right). View from the cross-shaped ventilation shaft (above).*

a spacious plaza to the south. On its east side a stream has cut a very deep ravine, making Toniná highly defensible.

The outer facing of the Acropolis and of the temples on each terrace was built up of horizontally placed limestone slabs that were once completely covered in stucco and painted. Surviving examples of stuccowork prove that its artists were as adept in this medium as those of rival Palenque. The most spectacular of these is the Frieze of the Dream Lords, discovered during Yadeun's excavations. It features a scaffold covered with quetzal feathers and hung with heads of sacrificed captives. Across it strides a weird skeleton with turtle shells as sandals and carrying a severed head; we know that this must have been a *way*, a spirit alter ego of an

Left: *A limestone sculpture of the Sun God at Toniná.*

Opposite: *A relief panel depicting a captive taken by a Toniná ruler.*

important king. In another part of the scaffold is our old friend Hunahpu, one of the Hero Twins of the *Popol Vuh*, above whom hovers the great Principal Bird Deity, who has removed part of Hunahpu's arm (exactly as in the K'iche' Maya story).

One of the largest ball courts of the Maya lowlands—far grander than anything at Palenque or Tikal—is sunk into the great plaza. Dedicated in 699, its playing area was embellished with the sculptures of six bound captives, all vassals of the Palenque state.

Toniná is renowned for its three-dimensional sculpture, a style unknown at any other Maya site except Copán. There are dated stelae for a succession of Late Classic kings, some of whom also took the solar title of K'inich. The greatest of these was probably Baaknal Chaak, who achieved many victories, the most famous one dating to AD 711, when he captured K'an Joy Chitam, king of Palenque. An amazing number of in-the-round sculptures are ample testimony that the Toniná rulers were as grimly bellicose as the kings of ancient Assyria. The captives are shown bound with ropes, and in one statue, about to be garroted. The hair was worn long, so the victims could be grasped by it with one hand and the head removed with an obsidian knife held in the other. Almost always, the jade ear ornaments were removed and a roll of cloth or jaguar skin pushed through the hole in the earlobe.

Perhaps Toniná's defensibility, its prowess in battle, and its access to flowing water enabled it to survive longer than any other city-state during the Great Collapse. In fact, the very last of the city's rulers managed to erect a monument in the year AD 904, long after most other Classic Maya capitals had already begun to be taken over by the ever-encroaching forest.

CITIES of the EAST

COPÁN

The most southeastern Maya city-state was Copán, situated in a fertile river valley amid the hills of western Honduras. Copán is famous among travelers for the beauty of its architectural sculpture in greenish volcanic tuff, for its magnificent ball court, for its Hieroglyphic Stairway (the longest Maya text yet known), and for the numerous stelae of its Classic rulers.

Copán was the first great Maya city that Stephens and Catherwood had ever seen. Arriving here on muleback in November 1839 following a horrific journey from the Caribbean coast, they were enormously impressed. As Stephens exclaims:

> No plans or drawings have ever been published, nor anything that can give an idea of that valley of romance and wonder, where . . . the genii who attended King Solomon seem to have been the artists.

Drenched by heavy thundershowers every twenty-four hours, plagued by mosquitoes and ticks, without decent medicines or adequate food, housed in a primitive thatched hut with a large local family, these two nevertheless managed to survey the ruins and accurately record monuments carved in a style that neither they nor anyone else in the Western world had ever seen or imagined.

One particular stone monument, placed directly in front of Copán's largest ruined pyramid, drew their attention:

> It is six feet square and four feet high, and the top is divided into twenty-six tablets of hieroglyphs, which beyond doubt record some event in the history of the mysterious people who once inhabited the city.

Copán's great Hieroglyphic Stairway is the longest Maya inscription known, with about 2,200 individual glyphs. The altar before it depicts a zoomorphic Flower Mountain.

We now know this great carved block as "Altar Q," and that its inscription records the founding of Copán; the sixteen figures extending around the sides of the block, each seated upon a hieroglyph, are (as Stephens surmised) a succession of the first sixteen of its rulers (there was to be only one more before the city passed from history).

Copán's founding father was Yax K'uk' Mo' (First Quetzal Macaw). Altar Q tells us that he was elevated to royal status on September 5, AD 426, and three days later he underwent an investiture ritual. There is every reason to believe that these events took place at distant Teotihuacán, the great imperial city of the Early Classic in the central highlands of Mexico. After a journey of 152 days, Yax K'uk' Mo' arrived at Copán, which he probably speedily incorporated into the *Pax Teotihuacana*. There had been a sedentary, native Maya people in the Copán Valley as early as 1200 BC (as Olmec-influenced pottery attests), and the foreign invader took a noblewoman of local origin as his queen.

That this warrior king pictured and named on an eighth-century stone monument actually existed has been triumphantly proved by a remarkable archaeological project. The entire southern part of central Copán is occupied by its Acropolis, which comprises three temple-pyramids, additional buildings on connected platforms, and two large courts.

At some time during the centuries between the abandonment of the site and the arrival of Stephens and Catherwood, the Copán River had leapt its usual banks (perhaps during a devastating hurricane) and had torn away structures along the east side of the Acropolis, leaving what Sylvanus Morley once claimed to be the greatest archaeological cross section in the world. Looking up at it from the river's edge, one can see that the ceremonial center of Copán is a gigantic palimpsest, floor piled on floor, building program on building program, reign after reign, until the city reached its final form.

Beginning as early as 1891, there have been large-scale excavation and epigraphic programs at the ruins of Copán by (among others) Harvard University, the Carnegie Institution of Washington, Pennsylvania State University, the Honduran Institute of Anthropology and History, Tulane University, and the University of Pennsylvania, as a result of which this is probably the best understood ancient city in all of Mesoamerica. During the past thirty years, three different projects have tunneled into the core of the Acropolis from its exposed river face, and revealed that the testimony of Altar Q, the stone that intrigued Stephens with its sixteen seated rulers, was absolutely factual, and not a Maya fantasy.

Right: *Temple 22 at Copán is dedicated to the Maize God. On its summit is a structure depicting the cloud-filled sky, supported by two aged divinities. The step at its foot rests on carved skulls depicting the Underworld.*

Overleaf: *View of the magnificent ball court of Copán, looking toward Stela 2. This is the third successive stage of the structure, completed in the reign of Waxaklahun Ubah K'awiil.*

One of these exploratory tunnels reached the interior base of Temple 16, Copán's long-lived State Temple, and encountered the tomb of the Founder himself, Yax K'uk' Mo', the foreigner from a distant land. On Altar Q he is depicted with a shield carefully obscuring his right arm, and an analysis of his skeleton indicated that this arm had been deformed from a badly healed fracture incurred in battle. Above the small temple that he had built in Teotihuacán style was an even more splendid tomb of an individual rightly considered by the University of Pennsylvania team as the Founder's spouse.

The dynasty established by Yax K'uk' Mo' had an almost unbroken succession of kings extending to the very last days of the city; they were responsible for the rebuildings, additions, and expansions that resulted in the Copán we see today. In the early sixth century, the seventh king (known by the modern nickname Waterlily Jaguar) oversaw a major expansion of the Acropolis, and most of these rulers added to and expanded the State Temple, each addition paying homage to the man deeply buried beneath it, Yax K'uk' Mo', the "First Quetzal Macaw" lord. The most spectacular of these later structures was the work of the tenth ruler, Moon Jaguar, who reigned from 553 to 578. Called Rosalilla by Honduran archaeologist Ricardo Agurcia, who discovered and excavated it, this is a buried temple-shrine dedicated to the Founder, extraordinarily complete because it had been covered by a later structure, its façade ornamented with brilliant polychrome stuccoes emphasizing the hybrid quetzal-macaw and the Sun God.

Tame scarlet macaws can still be seen at the entrance to the archaeological park at Copán.

Copán's longest-reigning ruler was its twelfth king, Smoke Imix (628–95); on Altar Q, he sits atop a glyph showing that he was a "5 K'atun Lord," that is, he had survived into his eighth decade—a Maya *k'atun* being a period of just under twenty years. This was a kind of golden age for Copán, its people, and especially the vast number of sculptors, architects, and scribes that must have been assembled there. Smoke Imix was largely responsible for the Great Plaza in the north half of the city center, a huge venue for public events, and a large number of monuments were carved and dedicated in his reign: ten stelae and four altars.

Smoke Imix began the construction of Temple 26, 125 meters (410 feet) to the north of Temple 16; this was to be his funerary temple-pyramid, and his richly stocked tomb is within it. He was accompanied by a sacrificed child and by the paraphernalia of a working scribe, including ink containers and the decayed remains of a codex (folding-screen book). Also placed in the tomb were ceramic effigies of the twelve kings who had preceded him.

Right: *Looking down on the players in Copán's ball court were structures fronted by mosaic sculptures of gigantic macaws, potent symbols in Copán's history.*

Overleaf: *Copán stelae. Second from left, Stela 2, with an inscription from the reign of Smoke Imix, the long-lasting seventh-century king. The other three are portraits of Waxaklahun Ubah K'awiil, erected before he was captured and beheaded in AD 738.*

This powerful head at Copán depicts an ancient, wrinkled deity, perhaps one of the Grandfather or Grandmother figures who act as progenitors of gods and humans in the mythic epic the Popol Vuh.

This man was clearly a scholar-king. It has long been noted that martial iconography is a rarity in the public sculpture of Copán; unlike most lowland Maya cities, these kings almost never display themselves garbed as victorious warriors, taking or trampling captives. The Altar Q portrait of Yax K'uk' Mo' is an exception, but his small shield must have been placed on his arm to cover up his deformity. Only near the close of Copán's long history, in reliefs on the top of Temple 11, do we see royal warriors.

This makes me wonder about the role of Copán within the Classic Maya world. How is it that in spite of constant acts of aggression between various polities, and the vicious treatment given defeated kings and their retinues, complex elements of higher culture—the gods, the rituals, the writing, and the calendric system in which this culture is expressed—are reasonably similar throughout? How could this be, unless there were some place or city where the various bearers of this culture, regardless of what city-state they came from, could meet and discuss matters of high import, and be protected from retribution. Copán may have played a role similar to that played by Delphi among the fractious ancient Greek cities.

One of these matters would have been the lunisolar calendar and the true length of the tropical year. It was an issue of great importance, as the official Maya year had only 365 days instead of the approximately 365¼ days that it takes the earth to orbit the sun. Significantly, it was in AD 682, during the reign of Smoke Imix, that Copán astronomers arrived at a formula that adjusted for this discrepancy, calculating that 149 moons equals 4,400 days, which means in our terms that a lunation averages 29.53020 days, remarkably close to what modern astronomers have determined it to be. This formula soon spread throughout all the contending powers in the Maya realm.

For modern visitors to Copán, the ruler who is most impossible to ignore is the next king, the unfortunate Waxaklahun Ubah K'awiil (18 Images of the God K'awiil). The Mayanists Simon Martin and Nikolai Grube rate his reign, from AD 695 to 738, as the acme of Copán's prosperity. He embellished the Great Plaza with seven self-portraits, in-the-round stelae carved in volcanic tuff and then lightly stuccoed and painted. These show the king in various guises, most strikingly in the jade bead–ornamented sarong and maize headdress of the Maize God, but also as local deities, including one who was a spirit called Mo' Wits (Macaw Mountain). These glorious sculptures were lovingly drawn by Catherwood in the magnificent lithographic portfolio that he published in 1844. The great king's sculptors were on an aesthetic par with the great stucco and limestone relief artists of Palenque.

Another of Waxaklahun Ubah K'awiil's achievements was building a new temple (Temple 26) on top of the one containing the tomb of his predecessor, Smoke Imix. In front of this new structure he began Copán's justly famous Hieroglyphic Stairway, but failed to complete it to the top for reasons that will shortly become apparent.

Adjacent to this structure he had constructed Temple 22, in its own right a masterpiece uniting great architecture with outstanding architectural sculpture in a stunning iconographic program. Temple 22 represents a major and ancient Mesoamerican concept concerned with the creation of the world, gods, and men—the Mountain of Sustenance, where the gods had hidden maize, the pan-Mesoamerican staff of life. We know that this temple-pyramid is a mythic mountain, as the corners of each tier are monster faces standing for the hieroglyph *wits*, "mountain." Within the temple on the summit, surrounding an inner doorway, is a sculptured tableau of the layers of the universe, with skulls below and two-directional gods holding up the heavens, in which cloud scrolls undulate. At one time, the upper walls were crowned with beautiful busts of the young Maize God, singing with half-open mouth and with one hand raised as though in blessing.

In its final form the ball court of Copán, one of the finest in existence, is also the legacy of this king. Strategically situated between the Great Plaza and the Court of the Hieroglyphic Stairway, it must have been a key venue in the ceremonial life of the city. Down its central axis, and set into the floor of the court, are three round boundary markers depicting pairs of ballplayers; one of these markers depicts Waxaklahun Ubah K'awiil facing off against an Underworld god, as though he were reenacting the role of his Maize God ancestor.

But was the ball court the only place in the city where this game was played? Many Late Classic Maya painted vases depict the rubber-ball game being played not in the standard I-shaped court, but against a set of stairs. In both the West and East Courts of Copán, adjacent to three major temple-pyramids, there are sets of three markers—square instead of round—that may well have been used to mark out playing areas like those in the ball court itself, with the rubber ball being bounced off stairways. In fact, the more we know about this important feature of Maya culture, the more we realize that there was not just one, but many kinds of ball games.

The Long Count date corresponding to April 29, AD 738, was an "Ides of March" event for Waxaklahun Ubah K'awiil. The small city of Quiriguá lies almost due north of

Opposite: *The four sides of Altar Q (dedicated in AD 776) depict Copán's first sixteen kings. Its upper surface, first described and pictured by Stephens and Catherwood, recounts the arrival from someplace in the west of Yax K'uk' Mo', the first king.*

Overleaf: *Four of the twelve clay incense burners from the deeply buried tomb of Copan's twelfth ruler, Smoke Imix. All are presumably royal portraits; on the far left is the first, Yax K'uk' Mo', with his "goggle" eyes. AD 695.*

Copán, across a low sierra in the valley of the Motagua River. From its founding in AD 426, its ruler had always been a vassal of Copán. The importance of this client state probably stemmed from the fact that the Classic Maya obtained all of their precious green jade from the riverbed of the Motagua and from the Sierra de las Minas to its north. However, on that fateful day, K'ak' Tiliw Chan Yopaat (Fire-burning Sky Lightning God), the current lord of Quiriguá, attacked Copán and captured its king, beheading him six days later. Subsequent to this, Quiriguá flourished under K'ak' Tiliw Chan Yopaat; though its architecture remained small-scale and undistinguished, its sculptors erected giant sandstone stelae with hieroglyphic inscriptions of an unsurpassed complexity and beauty.

In spite of this enormous setback, the Copán dynasty was reestablished, and life went on in the city. In AD 744 its fifteenth ruler was inaugurated. Under his leadership, the upper part of the Hieroglyphic Stairway was completed and Temple 26 achieved its final form. He was also responsible for Temple 11, and archaeologists suspect that his tomb lies somewhere within it.

The last Copán ruler of note was the sixteenth, Yax Pasah Chan Yopaat (First Dawn Sky Lightning). It is he who takes the scepter of office in 763 from the Founder on Altar Q, and during his reign the ceremonial part of the city reached the form that we see today, including the State Temple. It seems as though his authority over Copán's people was by no means as strong as that of his pre-Conquest predecessors, for in the northeast suburbs of the city lavish courts inhabited and administered by the higher nobles had sprung up. A few of these had magnificent "hieroglyphic benches"—thrones beautifully carved with astronomical and sacred figures. One of these complexes, in the group known as "Las Sepulturas," was the court of a very high-ranking royal scribe; besides an interior bench of the kind described above, the busts of scribal gods holding brush pens and conch-shell ink containers were placed in niches in the façade.

But Copán's days as a great Classic city were numbered. There is one last, pathetic monument—an unfinished square block—listing the accession of one Ukit Took' in the year AD 802. After that, silence. Yet the Copán Valley is exceptionally fertile, and lack of drinking water through drought, always a threat in the southern lowlands, could not have been a factor here. The kings and their courts disappeared, but the farming population stayed, right through to the Early Postclassic period (AD 925–1200) in fact, as finds of pottery of that period have proved. Whatever caused the downfall of Yax K'uk' Mo's dynasty was more likely to have been a political cataclysm than an ecological disaster.

This limestone tenon head from a Copán building depicts Chahk, the god of rain and lightning; from his head rises a cormorant-like bird with a fish in its beak.

MAYA RENAISSANCE in the NORTHERN LOWLANDS

In one of the greatest tragedies of ancient times, the Classic cities of the southern lowlands declined and were abandoned, one by one, throughout the ninth century, and this vast region largely reverted to rain forest. This sad story is revealed not only in the obvious decay through neglect of each city's monumental architecture, but more accurately in the failure of city after city to erect stone monuments dated in the Long Count system. There have been many hypotheses put forward to account for this cataclysm, the most compelling being agricultural collapse triggered by three brutal, multiyear droughts known to have occurred between AD 760 and 910. But the downfall of great civilizations, like that of the Roman Empire, is usually the result of multiple causes. By AD 800, Maya populations in the area had increased enormously, resulting in widespread deforestation and severe erosion. Warfare between the city-states had reached a crescendo, evidenced by jerry-built defensive walls hastily thrown around a few city centers. And the inhabitants of the Classic city of Aguateca were forced to flee their palaces and homes before unknown invaders burned the city to the ground.

Río Bec is actually a collection of fourteen small and loosely connected single (or at most two) buildings in a region so covered with rain forest that the most important group was lost for decades after its original discovery.

The leading Maya archaeologist of the twentieth century, Sir Eric Thompson, posited that uprisings and revolutions had finally toppled the dynastic ruling class. There is no lack of evidence for this: very few Classic stelae and other monuments have escaped breakage and vandalism, the figures of kings, queens, and nobles often have their eyes and mouths defaced (including the individuals in the Bonampak murals), and not one codex (bark-paper folding-screen book) has survived from the Classic, although the great cities once probably had whole libraries of them.

But somewhat farther north, and especially in the northern third of the Yucatán Peninsula, there was a remarkable flowering of Maya civilization during the ninth and tenth centuries, in what we now call the Terminal Classic, which endured until about AD 925. Ascribed to this brief period, especially in the Puuk area of the northwest, are a number of the greatest buildings ever created by the Maya, some of which have influenced a generation of architects of our own age. Concurrently, several northern cities with far older roots, such as Edzná in Campeche and Cobá in Quintana Roo, continued to flourish; and one—Ek' Balam in far northern Yucatán—astounds us with its spectacular artistry in three-dimensional stuccowork. It has been plausibly suggested that the droughts that supposedly brought the downfall of the southern Maya city-states were far more localized than had been thought, and had little effect on the north.

One great problem in dealing with all of these "cities of the north" has been the relative paucity of readable—and datable—inscriptions. Compared to southern cities, with the notable exceptions of Edzná and Cobá, they erected very few stelae or other dated monuments—often none at all—and those that were carved are often highly eroded because of the poor grade of limestone used. A further problem of legibility arises from the sad fact that few of their scribes and artists who worked with stone were very good calligraphers, compared to their peers in Palenque or Copán. We thus know all too little about northern dynasts other than the ones who lorded it over Ek' Balam (with its remarkable painted inscriptions).

The true iconographic and religious meaning of many Maya temples in the northern lowlands was discovered in 1987 through the decipherment of a single hieroglyph by the then-young epigrapher David Stuart. This was a sign that superficially looked like *Kawak* (one of the twenty day signs of the ritual calendar), but it had a cleft top and a foliated form. In its larger, more pictorial guise it displayed a cloven, zoomorphic stone head with an elongated upper lip, and Maya scholars began to call this the "Kawak Monster." Through a study of phonetic substitutions used by the Maya scribes, Stuart found that it was actually to be read as *wits*, the Maya word for "mountain."

In its larger sense, this zoomorphic being was not just any old mountain, but an embodiment of a solar paradise, the place of the Sun God, where the souls of kings, nobility, and brave warriors went to live forever, delighting in the divine perfume exhaled by flowers, the musical sounds uttered by lovely tropical birds, and the precious jades and gentle raindrops falling from above. Thanks to iconographic research by Karl Taube, pictorial representations of this Flower Mountain (*nichte' wits*, in Maya) are now known in the Maya lowlands from the Late Preclassic until the Spanish Conquest; the concept itself is even more widespread in the Americas, extending into central Mexico and even among the Pueblo peoples of the American Southwest.

This concept probably arose first among the Olmec, but later became elaborated among the lowland Maya, who, it will be recalled, live in a karstic limestone environment, in which caves and other solution cavities abound. Not surprisingly, Flower Mountain, as it appears in Maya art and architecture, has its own mouth, depicted as a vast reptilian maw set with great fangs—this is the cave of the living mountain mass, from which is emitted the breath of the gods and the ancestors who dwell in it. Aztec origin myths tell us something else about Flower Mountain, which they called *Tonacatepetl*, or "Mountain of Our Sustenance." In it the gods had hidden maize, the staff of life, along with other food plants. In one version of the story, Quetzalcoatl (Feathered Serpent), brings out the corn seeds to the upper world. It is myths of this sort that probably explain why, in the now-famous murals of San Bartolo, the Maize God and his retinue stand upon a feathered snake that has apparently brought them out from a cave inside Flower Mountain (see page 15).

A faulty understanding of Maya iconography by several earlier generations of scholars led to a serious misidentification of the so-called "long-nosed gods" on buildings in great centers like Uxmal, Kabah, and Chichén Itzá as the rain deity Chahk, rather than as multiple heads of Flower Mountain. What misled scholars such as the great German Mesoamericanist Eduard Seler is that in the very Late Postclassic Madrid Codex, the rain god's upper lip has been drawn out into a nose-like curlicue, a feature of Chahk unknown in Classic times and earlier.

RÍO BEC STYLE

Situated about 45 kilometers (28 miles) northeast of Calakmul—less than a day's march from that once-powerful capital—is a compact region enclosing a plethora of Terminal Classic sites in what has been known as the Río Bec style. This architecture is characterized by elaborate, almost baroque building façades of stone and stucco representing Flower Mountain and its reptilian cave; one entered the temple interior through a doorway lined with gigantic fangs. The Río Bec temple often consists of a low and functional—or range-type—religious structure, flanked by two soaring "false towers." With their high roof crests, these towers clearly imitate the major temple-pyramids of Tikal, but their stairways cannot be climbed and their doorways are illusory. They are unique in the pre-Columbian New World.

RÍO BEC

Río Bec, which gave its name to this architectural style, consists of twelve separate building complexes and has been known to archaeologists since its discovery in 1907 by the French explorer Maurice de Périgny.

Façade of a Río Bec building. The "checkerboard" panels flanking the doorway are typical of this architectural style.

XPUHIL

Only 20 kilometers (12 miles) to the north of Río Bec is the very similar Xpuhil, whose towers can be seen from the modern highway that crosses the peninsula from Chetumal on the Caribbean, west to Escárcega. Because of its proximity to this east–west highway, Xpuhil is the most-visited ruin in the Río Bec area. Nearby is a reed-covered waterhole that gave its name to the site (*Xpuhil* means "Place of the Cattails").

Structure I at Xpuhil. Terminal Classic. The characteristic twin "false towers" are visible on either side of a multiroomed building, but at the back, and obscured by the left-hand tower, is a far taller and better-preserved one. As usual, the towers are solid and therefore—like the "stairs"—nonfunctional.

CHICANNÁ

Just southwest of Xpuhil is Chicanná, with its enormous and befanged doorway leading into Flower Mountain.

Left: *Frontal view of the façade of Structure II, Chicanná. Note the upper teeth of a monster's mask.*

Opposite: *Structure XX, with stacked Flower Mountain masks on one corner.*

Overleaf: *West side of Structure II at Chicanná's Group A. The central façade is a symbolic Flower Mountain and the entrance is a cave with a gaping monster mouth.*

HORMIGUERO

Some 16 kilometers (10 miles) southwest of Chicanná is the beautifully preserved Hormiguero. Like many Maya sites in the southern lowlands, Hormiguero was first seen by *chicleros*—tappers of chicle latex for the chewing-gum industry. They reported buildings with stone doors that could close, and rooms from which strange noises emanated. Scientific exploration of Hormiguero began with the Carnegie Institution expedition of 1933.

The great monster-mask doorway on the south side of Hormiguero's Structure II, the largest building at the site.

Left: *View of Structure II, Hormiguero. The false towers on either side are sham temples, perhaps based on Tikal's facing Temples I and II.*

Right: *Looking back along the same façade.*

BECÁN

Becán lies in the midst of this cluster of Río Bec sites. Its somewhat more complex history begins in the Late Preclassic and flourishes in the Early Classic, during the Teotihuacán *imperium*, when its center was enclosed by an enormous moat and palisaded rampart. As there are no inscriptions at Becán (nor at any other Río Bec site), we have no idea who the enemy might have been to warrant such defensive works. By the Terminal Classic, Río Bec–style buildings were being put up, and the city managed to survive until the Late Postclassic period.

All of the Río Bec sites are in such close proximity to Calakmul that it seems inconceivable that they were not within Calakmul's political grasp, which exerted its power more widely than any other Maya city-state.

Right: *In the distance rises Structure IX, the principal temple-pyramid at Becán.*

Overleaf: *Panoramic view of Becán's East Plaza. On the right is the entrance to the city, passing through the defensive moat and earth rampart.*

Left: *A residential building at Becán.*

Above: *An Early Classic stucco relief on a Becán substructure; the face of a ruler peers out from the jaws of a composite monster.*

CHENES

TABASQUEÑO

Moving 90 kilometers (56 miles) north in the modern state of Campeche, one arrives at the cities of Terminal Classic "Chenes" style, derived from the number of contemporary Maya villages and towns in the area with names that end in *-chen*, "well." Chenes architecture closely resembles that of the Río Bec sites, featuring buildings, façades, masks, and gaping doorways all symbolizing Flower Mountain and its cave entrance, but lacking the false towers. Sites like Tabasqueño and Hochob also have an affinity with the great cities of the Puuk region, which they border on the south.

Opposite: *Stacked Flower Mountain masks on the corners of Structure I at Tabasqueño.*

Right: *Structure I's monster-mouth entrance.*

HOCHOB

Below: *The ornate façade of the main temple at Hochob.*

Opposite: *Two Hochob temple-pyramids with roof combs.*

THE PUUK CITIES

Stephens and Catherwood never did see the forest-shrouded ruins of Río Bec and the Chenes; until de Périgny's 1907 expedition, they would have been known only to the region's *chicleros* (chicle gatherers) and occasional hunters. But they did know the great Terminal Classic sites among and to the south of the Puuk hills of northwest Yucatán, and marveled. Here is what Stephens said on his first view of the beautiful structures of Uxmal:

> The place of which I am now speaking was beyond all doubt once a large, populous, and highly civilized city, and the reader can nowhere find one word of it on any page of history. Who built it, why it was located on that spot, away from water or any of those natural advantages which have determined the sites of cities whose histories are known, what led to its abandonment and destruction, no man can tell.

Certainly lack of water—for drinking, washing, cooking, and many other purposes—was a major problem for the inhabitants of the Puuk cities. Moving from south to northwest over the Yucatán Peninsula, the long winters between rainy seasons become increasingly dryer. In the near absence of standing water, the solution was to excavate down through the hard limestone and hollow out a *chultun*, a bottle-shaped cistern into which the summer rains were funneled. Each residential group in a Puuk settlement had at least one *chultun*; the city of Sayil, for instance, had more than three hundred.

The full moon illuminates the front of the House of the Magician temple-pyramid at Uxmal.

So what could have been the attraction of this somewhat desiccated area to the Maya? The answer is that Puuk soils were remarkably fertile, and maize agriculture could flourish. In fact, modern site surveys have shown that even the great Puuk sites were low-density "green cities," with garden plots and even maize fields existing almost contiguous to ceremonial structures.

Puuk architecture is generally agreed to be the most splendid ever produced by the Maya, and had an influence that has reached far beyond its time and place, most notably in the Mayan Revival style of early-twentieth-century American and British architects like Frank Lloyd Wright and Robert Stacy-Judd. Unlike the temple structures of the southern lowland cities, in which relatively rough stone blocks were held by a cement and rubble core and then given a thick coat of plaster, Puuk buildings were faced with a stone veneer of precisely cut squares, Flower Mountain masks, multiple "bound columns," and complex architectural mosaics formed of individually cut geometric elements. Each city has soaring temple-pyramids, but most Puuk structures are range-type buildings with multiple rooms. In some sites, room entrances are often divided by one or two standing columns, and upper façades have long lines of false columns bound with horizontal bands.

The Palace at Kabah at sunset.

UXMAL

The four best-known Puuk sites (and the most visited) are Uxmal, Kabah, Sayil, and Labná. Uxmal is undoubtedly the queen of Puuk cities. Visitors since the days of Stephens and Catherwood have been awed by its Governor's Palace, placed on its own great, square platform with a commanding view of the site as a whole. Here is what Stephens had to say about its highly complex mosaic upper façade: "The designs were strange and incomprehensible, very elaborate, sometimes grotesque, but often simple, tasteful, and beautiful."

Like almost all Puuk buildings, its corbel-vaulted rooms are unusually tall and spacious, and as tradition says, probably did house the ruler and his court, or at least give them offices! According to those few Uxmal monuments with hieroglyphic texts, the king was named Lord Chahk, and he reigned about AD 900. We know little about his history, but it was certainly he who was responsible for most of Uxmal's architectural glories.

Other buildings are equally stunning, masterpieces of precision masonry and architecture. The so-called Nunnery Quadrangle (there is no real record of the ancient Maya ever having had orders of nuns!) consists of four rectangular, single-story range-type buildings facing each other across a courtyard. The upper façade of each emphasizes a different theme; for example, the North Building has (or had) goggle-eyed masks of the ancient Teotihuacán war god, the West Building features Feathered Serpents and models of thatched Maya huts, and so forth. As for the function of these structures, it may well be that they were Young Men's Houses; among the Aztecs of central Mexico this type of building was called a *telpochcalli*, an academy in which young princes and nobles

The principal buildings at Uxmal, seen from the Great Pyramid. In the right foreground, stacked Flower Mountain masks.

received instruction in statecraft, religion, military matters—a use that has been suggested for Bonampak's Temple of the Murals. But we really don't know.

Dominating the Nunnery Quadrangle on the east is the House of the Magician, a tall temple-pyramid; officiants coming from the Nunnery would have entered its upper temple through a vast, fang-girded portal, with stacked Flower Mountain masks on each side.

Some distance to the west of the Nunnery is the "Cemetery Group," unique to Uxmal among Terminal Classic Maya sites, as its low platforms are embellished on the front with reliefs of skulls, crossbones, and disembodied eyes (complete with their nerve stalks). Almost surely this quadrangle, along with the small temple structure on one side, were dedicated to human sacrifice and displays of severed heads.

The pierced roof comb of this multiroomed Uxmal building has given it the modern name Las Palomas (the dovecote). The corbel-vaulted arch on the left was the entrance to the compound.

Uxmal's massive House of the Magician temple-pyramid underwent five successive rebuildings during the Terminal Classic period, reaching the height of about 35 meters (115 feet) in its final stage. Of the two superimposed temple façades on top, the lower one is in pure Chenes style.

The House of the Magician
temple-pyramid, looking
north from the Governor's
Palace. These were probably
Uxmal's two most important
structures, the latter devoted to
royal administration, and the
former (perhaps) to the royal
ancestral cult. In contrast to
the southern Maya cities, in
Uxmal readable texts are at
a minimum, so we can only
guess as to the function of
these beautiful buildings.

Above: *The middle section of Uxmal's Governor's Palace, fronted by a double-headed jaguar throne. The palace's upper façade is an elaborate mosaic of pre-carved limestone blocks that continues around all four sides.*

Opposite: *One of a pair of rings that served as bull's-eye goals for the ball game, Uxmal.*

KABAH

The Puuk site of Kabah lies 18 kilometers (11 miles) to the south of Uxmal, and is connected to it by a *sakbe* (white road or causeway). At the terminus of this ancient highway is a freestanding arch, much like those through which visitors once entered Roman cities (except that the Maya arch is corbeled, rather than "true"). Kabah's most famous building bears the local Yucatec Maya name of Kotz' Poop, meaning "rolled-up mat," for reasons that elude me. It is another one-story range structure, with a frontal façade made up, from floor to roofline, of what are said to have been as many as four hundred Flower Mountain mosaic masks, although many have fallen away over the centuries. There is nothing quite like it elsewhere in the land of the Maya. Once fully polychromed, it must have been an amazing sight in ancient times. The interior steps leading to back rooms consist of the rolled-up "nose" of one of these masks. Four doorjambs of the Kotz' Poop feature relief scenes showing the same sinister-looking protagonist spearing an enemy and taking captives; this individual, who appears in other sculptures at Kabah, wears a padded-cotton war jacket, and has a short goatee and prominent cicatrices curving around his eyes and down his face. He must have been the warlike king of this important city, but we know neither his name nor his history.

With a façade composed entirely of Flower Mountain masks, Kabah's Kotz' Poop building is unique.

Left: *This is one of four sculptured door jambs that depict the same Kabah lord in his battle jacket aiming a spear at a rival warrior.*

Opposite: *This freestanding arch is positioned at the southern end of a sakbe, or causeway, linking Kabah to Uxmal.*

Overleaf: *On the left, Kabah's Palace; on the right, the Kotz' Poop.*

SAYIL

Another member of this quartet of great Puuk sites is Sayil, also visited by Stephens and Catherwood on their second voyage to Yucatán. Its most striking building is known as the Palace. Its three levels are termed "stories," but in reality each "story" is a long row of rooms set back and over the basic rubble core of the building. It was a huge structure, divided into two halves by its frontal stairway. Sayil's major buildings are positioned in a roughly north–south line, and are connected by a long *sakbe*. This is the only Puuk city that has been mapped in its entirety, with the inclusion of all residential groups; from this, it is estimated that the population of this Terminal Classic site might have totaled 10,000 persons, with an additional 6,000 residing in satellite communities.

Sayil has a number of carved monuments, most of them either very badly executed or much eroded (or both). A few are truly crude, depicting nude males with enormous, dangling phalli; by comparison with some of the reliefs at Palenque, these may be humiliated captives. However, there was at this time a sort of phallic cult in the Puuk area—Uxmal used to have a virtual forest of stone phalli, but these indecorous objects have been removed from tourists' eyes.

Below: *The majestic Palace of Sayil. Most of the building to the right of the stairway is still in ruins.*

Opposite: *Like most Puuk architecture, the corners of Sayil's structures feature Flower Mountain masks and bound pseudo-columns.*

LABNÁ

The fourth member is Labná ("old house"). In his portfolio of 1844, Catherwood published a particularly beautiful colored lithograph of Labná's most memorable feature—its great freestanding arch. Its face is framed on either side by mosaic stone reliefs of thatched Maya huts. Again, as at the other Puuk sites, there is a "Palace," in this case only two instead of three "stories," and range-type buildings that might also have been "Young Men's Houses." Towering over the city on the south is El Mirador (The Lookout), a lofty, much-ruined temple-pyramid. Causeways interconnect all these groups.

The cities of the Puuk survived until about AD 1000, and some, like Uxmal, were at least partially inhabited until the arrival of the Spanish invaders. The influence of its architectural style extended far and wide, and we will see its presence even at the great city of Chichén Itzá, over 80 kilometers (50 miles) to the east.

One of Labná's many multiroomed residential buildings. The rows of bound pseudo-columns on the façade are typical of Puuk architecture.

Left: *View of El Mirador (The Lookout), a tall temple-pyramid at Labná.*

Opposite: *Flower Mountain masks flank a vaulted passageway into a building compound at Labná. The long "noses"—actually stylized, snout-like upper lips—led early scholars to misidentify them as masks of the rain god.*

Left: *View through the vaulted passageway at Labná that is flanked by Flower Mountain masks (see page 175).*

Overleaf, left: *El Mirador, seen through a corbel-vaulted archway.*

Overleaf, right: *The lovely freestanding arch at Labná, almost exactly as it was pictured by Catherwood in the nineteenth century. Step-and-fret mosaics decorate its upper façade on this side. Mosaic stone reliefs of thatched Maya huts ornament the other side.*

EDZNÁ

This major Maya city is situated in a savannah-covered lowland far to the southwest of the Puuk, a region of exceptionally rich soil. Edzná was unusually long-lived, having been founded in the Late Preclassic (most likely around 400–300 BC), and was probably continuously occupied until as late as AD 1200, in the Early Postclassic. It is one more argument that the ninth-century "Great Collapse" was really confined to the cities of the southern lowlands, while the northern city-states enjoyed a renaissance.

A remarkable feature of Edzná was created in the Late Preclassic. This is a huge radial canal system with twelve arms that converge toward the Great Acropolis. Its function is unclear, but it certainly solved the water problem for the inhabitants, and could have been used not only to hand-irrigate surrounding cropland, but also to harbor fish. The scale of such an enterprise implies a great degree of political centralization at an early date. Edzná flourished during the Early Classic, when we find large stucco masks of gods flanking stairways, as in sites like Tikal and Kohunlich (see pages 38 and 54–55).

The star attraction of Edzná is its splendid Five-Storied Temple. This grand structure, probably built up over several centuries, is placed on an enormous square platform; together with smaller temples, the entire complex comprises the Great Acropolis. In its final form, the Five-Storied Temple is a Terminal Classic structure in Puuk style, and bears some

Edzná's Five-Storied Temple. The "stories" are an illusion, for each level actually rests on a solid rubble core. It may have served an administrative and residential function, as well as being the religious center of the city-state.

resemblance to the Palace at Sayil (see page 170). Its multiple rooms have suggested to some investigators that it served both an administrative and a residential function. Surprisingly, there are no fewer than thirty-two stelae and two carved lintels known for Edzná, but most inscriptions are badly eroded, so we really don't know who these administrators were. Perhaps future epigraphers will be able to make more sense out of this spotty historical record.

Temple buildings facing the Great Acropolis of Edzná.

EK' BALAM

General books on the ancient Maya published as late as the 1950s and 1960s (including my own) failed to mention a site called Ek' Balam (translated as "Black Jaguar" in some Colonial sources, but more likely in Classic times to have been "Jaguar Star"), or even show it on their maps. Since that time, we have come to realize that this city in the northeast third of Yucatán is one of the most distinctive and consequential polities of the Classic era, with a magnificent epigraphic record. In short, we now know the person who created Ek' Balam as it looks today. This site was occupied from Late Preclassic times well into the Colonial period (the Spanish priests even placed a Christian chapel in its main plaza), and the place name by which it is still known to local Maya is actually recorded in its hieroglyphic inscriptions. As a polity, it was called by the dynastic name of Talol.

The ceremonial-political center of Ek' Balam is not extensive in area—6 square kilometers (2.3 square miles)—but it contains some impressively large structures. It is girded by two concentric walls, almost surely defensive in purpose; visitors or people from the surrounding district could have entered it on the south through a masonry arch recalling those at Kabah and Labná. Facing the central plaza on the north is the enormous Acropolis; thanks to discoveries made by a team of Mexican archaeologists in recent decades, we now know that this was the palace of an immensely powerful king named Ukit Kan Le'k Tok'—and eventually his funerary monument. Until his accession in AD 770, Ek' Balam was a rather unprepossessing city. This man changed all of that; he was not only a *k'ul ajaw* ("holy king") of Talol, he was also a *kalomte*, a title somewhat akin to our "autocrat."

Near the summit of the Acropolis is the most astounding stucco bas-relief ever sculpted by the Maya. Heavily influenced stylistically by Chenes iconography, it is symbolically

View south from the Acropolis toward the Oval Palace, Ek' Balam. The extreme flatness of the Yucatán landscape is readily apparent.

a Flower Mountain, the "cave" of which is entered though a reptilian mouth, in this case surrounded on all four sides by huge fangs. This is truly three-dimensional stuccowork: in-the-round standing figures of royal youths, with feathered "backracks" like those worn by the young nobles in the Bonampak murals, are placed on either side of the upper panel. Left gleaming white by its makers, this great façade was preserved intact by being covered over on the death of Ukit Kan Le'k Tok'. Beautifully painted mural-texts indicate that the whole structure had its own proper name: Sak Xok Naah, "White House of Reading," surely a reference to the many texts painted on the walls of the rooms within.

Excavating through the fanged doorway to an inner room, the archaeologists came across Ukit Kan Le'k Tok's vaulted tomb, one of the most spectacular ever discovered in the Maya area. Upon his death at the beginning of the ninth century, the king was laid out with the usual array of vessels containing food and drink, a shell necklace in the shape of skulls, and a small gold frog almost surely imported from Panama – a most unusual rarity, since the Classic Mesoamerica had no metals at all (metallurgy only appears in the Postclassic, probably introduced by traders from Ecuador and Panama). Over the room containing his tomb is a capstone painted with the deceased king portrayed as the young Maize God, the same concept that one sees on Pakal's famous sarcophagus lid at Palenque.

Similarly painted texts on the capstones of other rooms within the structure show that his successors (and, presumably, descendants) continued to revere Ukit Kan Le'k Tok' as a deified ancestor through much of the ninth century. He was certainly the greatest sovereign in all of northern Yucatán in his day.

Right: *The great, white stucco frieze on the Acropolis summit at Ek' Balam, a unique masterpiece of Late Classic Maya art. The huge fangs at the entrance usher one into a Flower Mountain and the burial place of the city's kings.*

Overleaf: *Ek' Balam's ball court can be seen on the far right. The large building annexed to it may have been devoted to ceremonies involved with the ball game.*

COBÁ

Opposite: *One of Cobá's two ball courts, situated in the northwest part of the main site; it sports a pair of stone rings, a Central Mexican feature that was introduced into the Maya area during the Terminal Classic.*

Overleaf: *The Nohoch Mul (Great Mound) pyramid at Cobá is of Classic date but is incongruously crowned with a diminutive Late Postclassic temple.*

Every Maya city is different from every other, and Cobá is no exception. Located around and between five small lakes, a rarity in the northeast of the Yucatán Peninsula, it is made up of several discrete groups, all linked by a large number of *sakbe'ob*; all of these causeways taken together total over 150 kilometers (93 miles). An even longer *sakbe* leads 100 kilometers (62 miles) directly west to the site of Yaxuná. On a personal note, in 1948 I walked over a good part of this jungle highway to reach Cobá, then totally deserted except for occasional visits by Maya hunters in pursuit of game like deer and ocellated turkeys.

Cobá was founded about AD 100, perhaps by immigrants from the southern lowlands, as it always retained a strong resemblance to cities like Calakmul, although on a smaller scale. Most of what one sees at the site is Late Classic in date, but not easy to appreciate, as very few structures have been excavated or even restored. There are also carved stelae, once again in poor condition due to surface erosion. But three of them are indeed unusual, for they record the beginning of the present Maya era (August 13, 3114 BC, in our own calendar) from a starting point billions of years in the past, in what epigraphers have called the "Grand Long Count."

Shortly after the close of the eighth century, Cobá suffered the same kind of collapse that befell its counterparts farther south, and was abandoned. Almost six centuries later it was reoccupied by Late Postclassic Maya, most likely coming in from trading communities on the east coast. On top of Cobá's tallest pyramid (Nohoch Mul, "Great Mound")—probably by then in disrepair—they placed a small, simple temple, totally out of scale with the giant that supported it. In another group is another rather diminutive temple with hieroglyphic writing on its exterior that bears a close similarity to that on a surviving but very late codex (the Madrid Codex). Following the Spanish conquest, one hears of Cobá no more, until its rediscovery in the late nineteenth century.

TWILIGHT of the ANCIENT MAYA

The Maya renaissance in the north came to an end in the tenth century, when Yucatán became the target of a major military and cultural takeover by a foreign people. These invaders were the Toltec, Nahua speakers from the central Mexican *altiplano*, a people remembered and revered by the later Aztecs. The Toltec story begins with their capital, Tollan, "Place of the Reeds," now known to be the ruined city of Tula in the state of Hidalgo, northwest of Mexico City. Founded sometime after AD 900, according to native accounts Tollan was ruled by a man known to his people as Topiltzin Quetzalcoatl (Our Honored Ruler the Feathered Serpent). In 987, following a power struggle within the city, Quetzalcoatl was forced to leave Tollan with his followers, eventually setting off in a raft from the Gulf Coast for a land to the east.

The Maya of Yucatán informed Diego de Landa, Yucatán's first bishop, that in a *k'atun* that ended in AD 987, a great leader called K'uk'ulkan, "Feathered Serpent" in Mayan, arrived from the west, conquered Yucatán, seized the already established city of Chichén Itzá, and made it his new capital. This Toltec diaspora finished off the Puuk and other Terminal Classic cities, and so began the Postclassic era.

There are various native chronicles and Spanish commentaries from the Colonial period that deal with the northern lowlands during the Postclassic era, but these are often self-contradictory. The main problem lies with Maya chronology. By the close of the Terminal Classic, the Maya Long Count was no longer in use, replaced by the so-called Short Count: a period of about 256¼ years representing 13 *k'atuns* of slightly under 20 years each, with each successive *k'atun* being expressed by the day on which it ended (which was always the day Ajaw, prefixed by a number between 1 and 13). So, if something was said to occur in a K'atun 6 Ajaw, which particular K'atun 6 Ajaw was it? For this reason, late Maya history is filled with more ambiguities than the earlier part of the Maya story.

Muyil is strategically located only 12 kilometers (7 ½ miles) inland from the Caribbean coast, and was connected to the intense coastwise trade of late pre-Conquest times by a canal-lagoon system. The city had a long occupation; this temple-pyramid dates from the Classic period.

CHICHÉN ITZÁ

Designated by UNESCO as a World Heritage center, Chichén Itzá is the most visited archaeological site in the Americas. The name of this tourist Mecca means "Mouth of the Well of the Itzá," a reference to the enormous, circular cenote, or deep natural sinkhole, that lies in its northern sector, and to the Itzá, a people who had moved into the by then abandoned Chichén (as we shall henceforth call it) in the thirteenth century.

Chichén's impressive structures have been known since the Spanish invasion, when the conquistador Francisco Montejo the Younger tried to found his own *Ciudad Real*, or "Royal City," in their midst; but he and his soldiers were eventually thrown out by the local Maya. Chichén was visited and described in some detail by Bishop Landa in his "Account of the Things of Yucatán"; and the city is also given a prominent place in native Maya sources of the Colonial period. During the Early Postclassic, it had become the capital of Yucatán and at that time was probably the largest city of Mesoamerica.

The first serious explorers to visit Chichén were Stephens and Catherwood, on their second voyage to the land of the Maya. Others followed throughout the nineteenth century, most notably the French explorer and photographer Claude-Joseph Désiré Charnay, who was the first to point out the strong similarity between Chichén's buildings

The great four-sided Castillo of Chichén Itzá, dedicated to the worship of the Feathered Serpent god, K'uk'ulkan. It was built around AD 900–1100 in two stages; the first temple-pyramid is completely enclosed within the later one and can only be reached by excavator's tunnels. The style of both structures was introduced by Toltec invaders from central Mexico.

and sculptures and those of Tula, Hidalgo, 1,125 kilometers (700 miles) to the west as the crow flies. Long-term excavations and reconstruction began in 1913 with the Carnegie Institution of Washington, led by the ebullient Sylvanus Morley until 1930, when Carnegie's interests turned toward the great Classic sites of the southern Maya lowlands. Other programs have since been under the auspices of Mexico's National Institute of Anthropology and History (INAH).

In spite of the immense size of this site and its overwhelming importance to Maya history, Chichén is very poorly known archaeologically. Unlike great Maya cities such as Tikal and Calakmul, or even Mexican ones like Tula and Teotihuacán, Chichén has never been mapped in such a way that we can talk about it as an inhabited city of known extent; the dating, relative or otherwise, of its great structures is often in doubt (radiocarbon dates are amazingly scarce); and there is still contentious debate about whether a Toltec period actually existed, with some extremists claiming that the Toltec are a myth, and that what looks "Toltec" is actually Late Classic Maya. Underlying all of this confusion is reluctance on the part of archaeologists to admit that any "Mexicans" could have invaded and subdued their beloved Maya—a mindset that we have already encountered with the Teotihuacán invasion during the Early Classic.

Putting all this debate aside, one can only conclude that there *was* a Toltec period at this site, that it can be dated to the Early Postclassic (AD 925–1200), and that it partially overlapped with the earlier Puuk-inspired occupation of Chichén. There is probably more stone sculpture here than at any other site in the Maya area of any period, and this is ample testimony for the introduction of Toltec traits originating in Tula. Chichén under Toltec domination was not only the greatest Mesoamerican city of its day, but also a splendid hybrid between an older yet still prestigious Maya culture and one stemming from Tula. The conquerors must have recruited some of the greatest architects familiar with the Puuk style, artists who could work in the Maya style, and priests imbued with the Maya gods and their iconography.

Completely new items abruptly appear in the archaeological record. One is gold and copper, hitherto unknown for the Maya; dredged up from the Cenote of Sacrifice were many copper bells, gold jewels from Panama, and a number of gold disks with repoussée scenes of Toltec warriors taking Maya captive and the like.

This fragment of a building corner, with its stack of Flower Mountain masks, is in Puuk style, and is evidence that Chichén was an important city even before the arrival of the Toltec.

Turquoise makes its first appearance, too; totally absent during the Classic, it was acquired by the Toltec from mines in the Pueblo country of Arizona and New Mexico, in exchange for tropical specialties like parrot and macaw feathers, as well as (we now know) cacao beans from which chocolate could be made. The reliefs on many square columns and door jambs at Chichén show Toltec warriors in their distinctive military costume, which included a pillbox-shaped hat fronted by a blue bird flying downward, padded protection on one arm, and a mirror-like back shield. These Mexican soldiers carry darts and spear-throwers, unlike the native Maya, who fought with thrusting spears. There are magnificent painted murals showing the Toltec army in active combat against the locals, armed with this weaponry. Above many reliefs depicting these clearly non-Maya warriors are their glyphic names, expressed in a system that is certainly non-Mayan but present at Tula; it has never been properly studied.

The strangest sculptures of this time are the recumbent statues called Chac Mools. They were first described and named at the end of the nineteenth century by the highly eccentric British-born couple Augustus and Alice Dixon Le Plongeon, who actually conducted a large-scale dig at the site. They claimed (who knows why) that these odd sculptures represented a Maya ruler by this name, which means "Great Claw," and the name has stuck. There is absolutely no Maya precedent for these sculptures, but they are found in western Mexico and notably at Tula, where one has a sacrificial knife strapped to one arm. They almost surely are associated with heart sacrifice, a practice introduced to Yucatán by the Toltec (the Classic Maya preferred decapitation). Chac Mools have had a long life into our own time, having been the direct inspiration for Henry Moore's renowned recumbent sculptures.

The Puuk (Terminal Classic) structures are concentrated in the southern part of the site, such as the so-called Nunnery, and its adjunct the Iglesia (Church). Here we find the usual Flower Mountain masks and other elements of Puuk architecture, but the Nunnery has an important set of stone lintels with long hieroglyphic texts. These describe such activities as fire rituals and include names known to us from Maya ethnohistoric texts, most importantly

This colonnade, adjacent to Chichén's Temple of the Warriors, was once covered with a flat roof, and is a type of architecture that was introduced by the Toltec from their capital city, Tula, in the central Mexican highlands.

what seems to have been the war leader K'ak'upakal (Fiery Shield). It used to be thought that these inscriptions indicated that Terminal Classic Chichén was governed by a triumvirate of equal partners, but that conclusion is now in doubt. We still do not know how the city was ruled. An unusual building usually ascribed to Terminal Classic Chichén is the Caracol, a circular structure placed on a flat platform, and named for the snail-like spiral stairway within it. It may have been dedicated to the Maya wind god but could also have functioned as an observatory, with sight lines that tracked the movements of the planet Venus against the horizon.

The great monument of Toltec Chichén is the world-famous Castillo; along with the Aztec Calendar Stone it is virtually an icon of Mexico. This nine-tiered, radial pyramid (the second to be built on the same spot) rises 29 meters (95 feet) above the Great Plaza; its four stairways are flanked by Feathered Serpent balustrades. Bishop Landa, an impeccable authority, affirms that it was dedicated to K'uk'ulkan. But it is an architectural hybrid: the rooms of the superstructure are corbeled (a technique unknown in the Mexican highlands), but the jambs of its doorways have reliefs of Toltec warriors.

Not far northeast of the Castillo is the Temple of the Warriors, a far grander version of Tula's principal temple; as with the Castillo, there is an earlier version of the temple within. After climbing the steps and passing by a Chac Mool, officiants entered the principal structure between Feathered Serpent columns. Inside, its walls (and the walls of the structure buried below) were painted with murals vividly depicting battle scenes and human sacrifice involving Toltec and Maya warriors. In front and to the south of the main temple are extensive, flat-roofed colonnades (a Tula specialty) with many hundreds of squared columns bearing reliefs on all sides of Toltec men at arms, some identified above with their names in Toltec glyphs.

The Great Ball Court—the largest known in Mesoamerica—is situated northwest of the Castillo. It is so vast and yet has such extraordinary acoustics that the conductor Leopold Stokowski once brought a symphony orchestra here to test them. The court has the usual I-shaped plan, with a stone ring carved with entwined Feathered Serpents set high on each wall; it is claimed that if and when the rubber ball with which the game was played passed through such a ring, the game was over, but this must have happened very, very rarely. Below, the sloping batters are carved with reliefs depicting teams of the contending players

The Castillo, viewed from one of Chichén's two dance platforms.

in a mixed Maya-Toltec style, with the leader of one side suffering decapitation. Atop one wall is the Temple of the Jaguars, its exterior covered with reliefs of prowling felines and coyotes, as in Toltec Tula; the interior once had a magnificent mural depicting with great sophistication a fierce battle between Toltec fighters and their Maya antagonists, but it is now in a sorry state of deterioration.

Adjacent to this ball court—actually one of four known at the site—is a rectangular platform carved on the sides with impaled skulls, surely the base of a *tzompantli*, or "skull rack," where the heads of sacrificed captives were skewered and displayed. Near it are two other stone platforms on which, according to Landa, farces and dances were staged.

Human sacrifice is also the theme of the Sacred Cenote, reached by a long causeway leading north from the Great Plaza. Several ethnohistoric accounts provide irrefutable evidence that this great natural sinkhole was the place where human victims were hurled to their deaths from Toltec times through the Spanish Conquest. From the deep muck that lies beneath its waters, underwater exploration has yielded a treasure trove in objects that had been thrown into the cenote as offerings through the ages: objects made out of copper, gold, jade, wood, flint (even sacrificial knives with wooden handles), and bowls filled with copal incense. Some of the jade objects are heirloom pieces from the Classic, but most of the finds are Postclassic in date.

The Temple of the Warriors at Chichén is a hybrid Toltec-Maya production that combines Puuk architectural elements with a Toltec prototype—Pyramid B at Tula. Reliefs of Toltec warriors are carved on all four faces of the square columns.

MAYAPÁN

By the thirteenth century, the compact, walled city of Mayapán had replaced Chichén Itzá as the capital of Yucatán and the northern Maya. The story of Mayapán revolves around the tangled history of the people called Itzá. According to one scenario, these despised foreigners, who were said to have spoken Yucatec Maya badly, had arrived from the Gulf Coast of Campeche at the then-deserted city of Chichén in a K'atun 4 Ajaw (AD 1224–44), and resettled it. They were led by a man who called himself K'uk'ulkan, which in those days must have been more a title than a personal name.

In a K'atun 13 Ajaw (AD 1263–83), one group of Itzá founded Mayapán, which is located about halfway between Mérida and the Puuk ruins to the south. A defensive wall completely encloses this miniature city, which covers only 6.5 square kilometers (2½ square miles). By 1283, the Kokom—the ruling lineage of the Itzá—held the rulers from the rest of Yucatán, and their families, as virtual hostages within the city walls, guaranteeing a steady flow of tribute into what was then the capital of the northern peninsula. The Carnegie archaeologists who completely mapped and studied Mayapán in the 1950s estimated a total population of between 10,000 and 12,000 people, although some have revised this upward to 15,000–17,000.

The city is completely devoid of streets and avenues, house groups being located almost haphazardly like those in the dispersed-urban cities of the Classic, but in a much

Circular buildings in Postclassic Yucatán, like this example at Mayapán, are believed to have been dedicated to Ehecatl, the wind god of central Mexico. In front, a Puuk-style Flower Mountain mask, probably brought to the site from a ruined Puuk city.

Left: *Detail of the Puuk-style Flower Mountain mask that stands in front of a Toltec-influenced circular building in Mayapán (see pages 206–7).*

Opposite (gatefold front): *The noble-class residential building on the left faces a plaza. On the far right is Mayapán's Late Postclassic Castillo, an imitation of the one at Chichén, and also known to have been reserved for the Feathered Serpent cult.*

smaller space. As this part of the peninsula is extremely arid and rocky, the inhabitants relied on water from an unusually large number of cenotes dotted among the compounds.

Mayapán is essentially a very small-scale version of Toltec Chichén, but both its art and architecture are shoddy compared to that of its great prototype. At its center is a four-sided, radial pyramid that we know from Bishop Landa was dedicated to K'uk'ulkan, the Feathered Serpent god. Other buildings in the central area include three round temples recalling Chichén's Caracol, probably dedicated to the worship of the planet Venus as the Morning Star, and perhaps also to the wind god (we know that among the Aztecs, the Feathered Serpent deity was lord of both). Flower Mountain masks are featured on the exteriors of some structures, but these may well have been removed from nearby Puuk ruins and reassembled by the city's architects.

Landa states that the dwellings of important lords were located near the city's ceremonial center, and the Carnegie excavations proved this to be the case. Within these colonnaded buildings and shrines were found effigy incense burners of fired clay, depicting various gods important to the Postclassic Maya such as the Maize God, the long-nosed deity who presided over trade and commerce, and the monkey-man god of scribes.

In a K'atun 8 Ajaw (AD 1441–63), the Itzá who still remained in Chichén abandoned it (Chichén was already falling into ruin when the Spaniards arrived). At the same time, the Kokoms who reigned over Mayapán were overthrown in an internal revolt, and Mayapán was also abandoned. What happened to the Itzá after these calamities? Most scholars believe the accounts describing a diaspora south to Lake Petén Itzá in northern Guatemala, where they founded a new capital on an island in the lake. This was Tayasal, the very last independent stronghold of the Maya; it was not to fall into the hands of Spanish forces until AD 1697.

Opposite (gatefold back):
Immediately east of the Castillo of Mayapán is a karge, a circular building that may have served as a temple of the central Mexican wind god, Ehecatl, and as an observatory for naked-eye observation of the moon and the planet Venus.

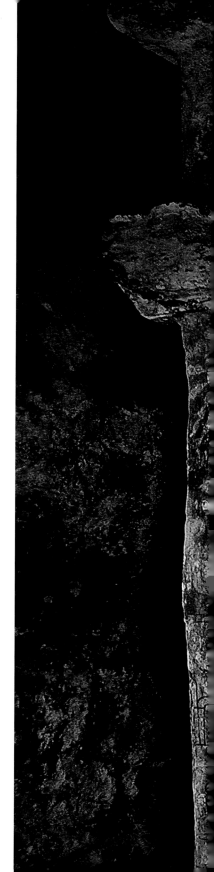

TULUM

Long-distance trade had been vital to the lowland Maya ever since the Late Preclassic, because many necessities for both royals and commoners in one or another city-state were not always available locally. These ranged from mundane but useful products like obsidian for weapons and tools, and salt (obtained either from seaside communities or from very rare salt springs), to more prestigious, elite commodities like jade, quetzal feathers, and cacao (chocolate beans). All during the Classic era the really important trade routes were overland, but this kind of internal commerce plummeted in importance at the time of the Maya Collapse.

However, by the Late Postclassic (after about AD 1200), a new mercantile pattern was established that was almost entirely coastwise. Merchants now traveled in huge, seagoing dugout canoes, paddling along a route that extended from the northwest coast of Honduras, up and around the Yucatán Peninsula, and down to the great international trading port of Xicallanco, where they would have met with their Aztec counterparts— and, of course, back again along the same route. There is reason to believe that valuable merchandise such as cacao traveled this way, and Mexican manufactures like copper bells. In August 1502, on his fourth and last voyage to the New World, while lying off the Bay Islands of Honduras, Columbus seized two of these merchant vessels, rowed by slaves. Aboard one, under a canopy, were the merchant and his family, and a large

The paintings in Tulum's Temple of the Frescoes are in a Late Postclassic "International Style," strongly influenced by the tradition of codex painting among the Mixtecs of Oaxaca.

cargo that included cast-copper ornaments and tools, finely woven textiles, and what the admiral's son called *almendras,* or "almonds." We know that the latter were cacao beans, but Columbus could never have grasped what they were used for, as he never actually touched upon the shores of Mesoamerica, where he might have discovered how chocolate was made and consumed.

The entire Caribbean coast of the peninsula is dotted with numerous Late Postclassic sites, most of them quite small and with fairly crude masonry structures thickly coated with lime plaster. They were probably all ports and depots for this maritime trade, as this coastline has a large number of bays—some of great size—and offshore cays that could have provided safe anchorage for long-distance merchants. Not far inland from these little ports were a few very ancient and still occupied centers such as Cobá, with its small, shoddy Late Postclassic temple placed atop a lofty pyramid of Classic date, and Muyil, a site with a millennium of history that benefited from its connection with this late pre-Conquest trade route through a channel that connected it with the Caribbean.

The gem among all of these late coastal sites is Tulum, located 130 kilometers (81 miles) south of the vacation Mecca of Cancún. This tiny, ruined settlement now receives tens of thousands of tourists annually. However, in December 1949, when I first laid eyes on Tulum (traveling there by a fishing boat hired on the island of Cozumel), the sign-in book kept by the Maya guardian had the names of only five other visitors that entire year. That part of the peninsula was then under the control not of the Mexican government but of independent Maya chiefs owing loyalty to the cult of the Talking Cross, a religion that once prophesied the eventual overthrow of the Whites and a return of the land to the Maya. The rise of Cancún and the so-called "Riviera Maya" has changed all that, and a small modern city now impinges upon Tulum.

The first explorers to bring Tulum to the attention of the world were, naturally, Stephens and Catherwood. In their day (March 1842), it was choked by almost impenetrable jungle vegetation, but undaunted, they worked on, mapping the site and drawing its major structures. Here is Stephens's ironic description of his companion attempting to draw one of Tulum's buildings (the Castillo), using his usual *camera lucida,* a box-like device that threw an accurate image on a ground-glass screen:

Preceding pages, left:
The seaward (east) side of the Castillo at Tulum. This view was probably seen by the conquistador Juan de Grijalva in May 1518, as he reconnoitered the Yucatán coast. He reported that this miniature city was as large as Seville.

Preceding pages, right: *Distant view of the Castillo, perched on a cliff overlooking the blue Caribbean. This tiny walled town participated in the long-distance, coastal trade system of the Late Postclassic Maya.*

Opposite: *The landward (west) side of the Castillo of Tulum. The general shoddiness of Tulum masonry was disguised by thick coats of plaster.*

Opposite the foot of the steps was a square terrace, with steps on all four of its sides, but the platform had no structure of any kind upon it, and was overgrown with trees, under the shade of which Mr. Catherwood set up his camera to make his drawing; and, looking down upon him from the door of the Castillo, nothing could be finer than his position, the picturesque effect being greatly heightened by his manner of keeping one hand in his pocket, to hide it from the attack of moschetoes [*sic*], and by his expedient of tying his pantaloons around his legs to keep ants and other insects from running up.

Tulum is a diminutive settlement (one can scarcely call it a "city") with a truly spectacular setting, perched upon a low cliff fronting the blue-green waters of the Caribbean. A small cove would have furnished some protection for trading canoes putting in to its shore. Enclosed on three sides by a defensive wall and on the fourth by the cliff, it probably never had a population larger than 500 to 800 people, living along a single "street" in thatched houses placed on low platforms. The Castillo is its most prominent structure, and it looks rather like a diminutive, crudely built version of Chichén's Temple of the Warriors. It is reached from the west, or land, side by a staircase, and one enters the vaulted rooms on top between two very eroded Feathered Serpent columns. On my first visit over sixty years ago, there was a Talking Cross—a dressed wooden crucifix—set up on a table in one of the rooms.

The most notable structure at Tulum is the two-storied Temple of the Frescoes. The walls of its rooms were once completely covered with murals, painted in a late, non-Maya mode apparently based upon the codices (folding-screen books) of the Mixtec of Oaxaca, in the Mexican highlands. Aptly called the "International Style," it was widely distributed among the late, pre-Conquest sites of southeastern Mesoamerica. The murals in this temple depict gods and goddesses engaging in various activities; one goddess grinds maize on a *metate* (stone quern), another carries small images of the rain god Chahk. The upper façade of another temple features a winged, diving deity in polychromed stucco, believed

Tulum's two-storied Temple of the Frescoes. Faces of the old Creator God are sculpted on the corners of the lower story.

by some researchers to be a star god. Other buildings are columned, single-story edifices that probably had flat roofs and served as elite residences. Some structures are little more than shrines hardly larger than a doghouse. All would have been scorned for their slipshod workmanship by the master architects who had built Chichén Itzá and the Puuk sites.

In May 1518, Diego Velásquez, Governor of Cuba (and an enemy of Hernán Cortés, future conqueror of Mexico), sent an expedition of four ships west to reconnoiter the island of Cozumel and the mainland coast opposite. Juan Díaz, one of the soldiers on the voyage, reported the following:

> We followed the shore day and night, and the next day towards sunset we perceived a city or town so large, that Seville would not have seemed more considerable nor better; one saw there a very large tower; on the shore was a great throng of Indians, who bore two standards which they raised and lowered to signal us to approach them; the commander did not wish it.

Setting aside the obvious—at that time Seville probably contained 60,000 souls!—this could only have been Tulum, the largest settlement along the coast during the Late Postclassic. If those natives had only known that these strange, bearded foreigners in their caravels were one day to effectively obliterate Maya civilization, they might not have made such a welcoming gesture.

On the left, the Temple of the Diving God at Tulum, an example of the poor construction prevalent in Late Postclassic times along the Yucatán coast, on the eve of the Spanish invasion. On the right is the Castillo.

GLOSSARY

ajaw Maya title meaning "king" or "lord."

atlatl Nahuatl (Aztec) word for a lever-like wooden tool for hurling darts or spears with great speed and force.

backrack An elaborate construction of wood and feathers worn on the backs of royal dancers.

celt A small polished axe of jade or other stone.

cenote Large, limestone sinkhole partly filled with water.

chultun Bottle-shaped pit cut into underlying limestone; used to collect water.

codex Latin word for a Maya book, made of bark paper folded in screen or accordion fashion, with individual pages coated with polished white gesso.

corbel arch Arch, roughly V-shaped in cross section, formed of overlapping courses of stone and capped with a flat stone.

Emblem Glyph A complex glyph identifying a named individual as a "Holy King" of a particular city-state.

Hunahpu One of the Hero Twins in the *Popol Vuh*, identified archaeologically by the black spots on his face and body.

INAH Acronym of Mexico's Instituto Nacional de Antropología e Historia.

k'atun Calendrical period of 20 *tuns* (7,200 days).

k'inich "Sun-eyed" or "sun-faced," a solar title taken by some Maya kings, especially at Palenque.

Long Count The day-to-day count of a Maya cyclical calendar made up of *bak'tuns, k'atuns, tuns, winals,* and *k'ins,* starting on a day in 3114 BC. It fell into disuse after the Classic Maya collapse in the late ninth and early tenth centuries.

Popol Vuh The "Book of Counsel" of the K'iche' Maya people, written down in early Colonial times. It contains the Maya Creation Myth in its fullest form.

Puuk A range of low hills in northwest Yucatán, and the name of an architectural style of the Terminal Classic.

Principal Bird Deity (PBD) The avian aspect of Itzamnaaj, the Maya creator deity.

sakbe "White road," a raised Maya causeway connecting cities, suburbs of cities, or temple complexes within a city.

Short Count Maya calendar in use during the Terminal Classic and Post-Classic Maya periods, based on a recurring cycle of 13 *k'atuns,* (about 256¼ years).

talud-tablero Architectural style originating in Teotihuacán, in which temple platforms consist of an oblong entablature (*tablero*) over a sloping batter (*talud*).

tzompantli Nahuatl (Aztec) name for the platform and upper framework that held the skewered skulls of sacrificed captives.

SELECTED BIBLIOGRAPHY

Barnhart, Edwin L. "Urbanism at Palenque." *The PARI Journal* 4, no. 1 (2003): 10–16.

Benavides Castillo, Antonio. *Edzná: una ciudad prehispanica de Campeche/Edzná: A Pre-Columbian City in Campeche.* Pittsburgh: Instituto Nacional de Antropología e Historia and the University of Pittsburgh, 1997.

Carrasco Vargas, Ramón, Verónica A. Vásquez López, and Simon Martin. "Daily life of the Ancient Maya Recorded on Murals at Calakmul, Mexico." *Proceedings of the National Academy of Sciences* 106, no. 46 (2009): 19245–49.

Canter, Ronald L. "Rivers among the Ruins: The Usumacinta." *The PARI Journal* 7, no. 3 (2007): 1–24.

Coe, Michael D. *The Maya.* 8th ed. London & New York: Thames & Hudson, 2011.

——. *Breaking the Maya Code.* 3rd edition. London and New York: Thames & Hudson, 2012.

Diehl, Richard A. *The Olmec Civilization.* London and New York: Thames & Hudson, 2004.

Estrada Belli, Francisco. *First Maya Civilization: Ritual Power in the Maya Lowlands before the Classic Period.* London: Routledge, 2011.

Fash, William L. *Scribes, Warriors and Kings: The City of Copán and the Ancient Maya.* London and New York: Thames & Hudson, 1991.

Folan, William J. "Calakmul," in *The Oxford Encyclopedia of Mesoamerican Cultures.* David Carrasco, ed. Vol. I (2001): 117–21.

Folan, William J., Ellen R. Kintz, and Laraine A. Fletcher, eds. *Cobá: A Classic Maya Metropolis.* New York: Academic Press, 1983.

Gendrop, Paul. *Los estilos Río Bec, Chenes y Puuk en la arquitectura maya.* Mexico City: Universidad Nacional Autónoma de México, 1983.

Golden, Charles, and Andrew Scherer. "Border Problems: Recent Archaeological Research along the Usumacinta River." *The PARI Journal* 7, no. 2 (2006): 1–16.

Grube, Nikolai, ed. *Maya: Divine Kings of the Rain Forest.* Cologne: Könemann, 2000.

Hansen, Richard D. "El Mirador, Guatemala: El Apogeo del Preclásico en el Área Maya." *Arqueología Mexicana* 11, no. 66 (2004): 26–33.

Harrison, Peter D. *The Lords of Tikal: Rulers of an Ancient Maya City.* London and New York: Thames & Hudson, 1999.

Houston, Stephen D., ed. *Function and Meaning in Classic Maya Architecture.* Washington, D.C.: Dumbarton Oaks, 1998.

Houston, Stephen D. "A Splendid Predicament: Young Men in Classic Maya Society." *Cambridge Archaeological Journal* 19, no. 2 (2009): 149–78.

Houston, Stephen D., and Takeshi Inomata. *The Classic Maya.* Cambridge, U.K.: Cambridge University Press, 2009.

Kowalski, Jeff Karl. *The House of the Governor: A Maya Palace of Uxmal, Yucatan, Mexico.* Norman: University of Oklahoma Press, 1987.

Kristan-Graham, Cynthia, and Jeff Kowalski. *Twin Tollans: Chichén Itzá, Tula, and the Epiclassic to Early Postclassic Mesoamerican World.* Washington, D.C.: Dumbarton Oaks, 2007.

Lacadena García-Gallo, Alfonso. "The Glyphic Corpus from Ek' Balam, Yucatán, Mexico." FAMSI (2004): http://www.famsi.org/reports/01057/section02.htm.

Lothrop, Samuel K. *Tulum: An Archaeological Study of the East Coast of Yucatan.* Washington, D.C.: Carnegie Institution of Washington, 1924.

Martin, Simon, and Nikolai Grube. "Maya Superstates." *Arqueología Mexicana* 48, no. 6 (1995): 41–46.

——. *Chronicle of the Maya Kings and Queens.* 2nd ed. London and New York: Thames & Hudson, 2008.

Miller, Mary E. *The Murals of Bonampak.* Princeton: Princeton University Press, 1986.

——. *Maya Art and Architecture.* London and New York: Thames & Hudson, 1999.

Miller, Mary E., and Karl Taube. *The Gods and Symbols of Ancient Mexico and the Maya.* London and New York: Thames & Hudson, 1993.

Prem, Hanns J., ed. *Hidden among the Hills: Maya Archaeology of the Northwest Yucatan Peninsula.* Acta Mesoamericana, no. 7. Bonn: Universität Bonn, 1994.

Sharer, Robert J., and Loa P. Traxler. *The Ancient Maya.* 6th ed. Palo Alto, Calif.: Stanford University Press, 2005.

Smyth, Michael P., Christopher Dore, and Nicholas Dunning. "Interpreting Prehistoric Settlement Patterns from the Maya Center of Sayil, Yucatan." *Journal of Field Archaeology* 22, no. 3 (1995): 321–47.

Stephens, John L. *Incidents of Travel in Central America, Chiapas, and Yucatan.* 2 vols. New York: Harper and Brothers, 1841.

——. *Incidents of Travel in Yucatan.* 2 vols. New York: Harper and Brothers, 1843.

Stuart, David, and George Stuart. *Palenque: Eternal City of the Gods.* London and New York: Thames & Hudson, 2008.

Tate, Carolyn E. *Yaxchilan: The Design of a Maya Ceremonial City.* Austin: University of Texas Press, 1992.

Taube, Karl A., "Flower Mountain: Concepts of Life, Beauty, and Paradise among the Classic Maya." *Res: Anthropology and Aesthetics*, no. 45 (2004): 69–98.

Tozzer, Alfred M., ed. *Landa's Relación de las Cosas de Yucatán.* Cambridge, Mass.: Peabody Museum of American Archaeology and Ethnology, Harvard University, 1941.

Velásquez García, Erik. "The Captives of Dzibanche." *The PARI Journal* 6, no. 2 (2005): 1–4.

Wauchope, Robert, ed. *They Found the Buried Cities: Exploration and Excavation in the American Tropics.* Chicago and London: University of Chicago Press, 1965.

Webster, David. *The Fall of the Ancient Maya: Solving the Mystery of the Maya Collapse.* London and New York: Thames & Hudson, 2002.

Yadeun, Juan. *Toniná: El laberinto del inframundo.* Gobierno del Estado de Chiapas, Mexico: Espejo de Obsidiana, 1993.

INDEX

ACKNOWLEDGMENTS

My deep gratitude to Professor Michael D. Coe for agreeing to collaborate with me on this project. It would not have been possible without his guidance; he supplied the selection of sites that he thought appropriate to include in the book. We were fortunate to be able to travel together throughout the Río Bec area, which Mike had not revisited for a number of decades. We share the gifts of curiosity and imagination, which have served both of us in our chosen fields of expression. This has resulted in a delightful give-and-take in the creation and interweaving of text and images. It has not only been the closest collaboration with an author that I have experienced on any of my books, but it has also been the beginning of a friendship with a kindred spirit. My thanks to my publisher Mark Magowan, who asked of me, while discussing our *Temples of Cambodia* project, "Do you think you might have any interest in doing a similar book on the Maya?" I laughed and told him that I had begun to do so in 2003. Many thanks to Sandra Klimt and Heather Graef for their invaluable contributions to the production of this book. My sincere appreciation to Jacqueline Decter for her discernment and wisdom in editing the book. I am deeply indebted to Dan Griffin of Merida for his knowledge of the Maya ruins throughout Mexico and Guatemala; he has been my guide and companion on a number of journeys through all of those sites. My thanks to Mike Valladares for performing a similar role during my travels to Copán Ruinas in Honduras, and to Flavia Cueva for her gracious hospitality at her lovely Hacienda San Lucas. My thanks also to Nikon and Nik Software for their continued support. My sincere gratitude to my dear friend and mentor Morrie Camhi, whose spirit sustains and supports me in my photographic endeavors.

—Barry Brukoff

I would like to thank Mark Magowan, Barry Brukoff, and Helen Ibbitson Jessup for suggesting that I participate in the creation of this unique project.

—Michael D. Coe

First published in the United Kingdom in 2012 by Thames & Hudson Ltd, 181A High Holborn, London WC1V 7QX

Photographs copyright © 2012 Barry Brukoff
Text copyright © 2012 Michael D. Coe
Copyright © 2012 The Vendome Press

All Rights Reserved. No part of this publication may be reproduced or transmitted in any form or by any means, electronic or mechanical, including photocopy, recording or any other information storage and retrieval system, without prior permission in writing from the publisher.

British Library Cataloguing-in-Publication Data
A catalogue record for this book is available from the British Library

ISBN: 978-0-500-97040-9

Printed and bound in China

To find out about all our publications, please visit **www.thamesandhudson.com**.
There you can subscribe to our e-newsletter, browse or download our current catalogue, and buy any titles that are in print.

Endpapers: *A stucco relief on the Toniná Acropolis. The meaning of the symbolism, which includes sunken handprints, remains elusive.*

Page 1: *Lid of polychrome bowl, ca.* AD *500, excavated in Becan, Campeche, Mexico. Depicted is a composite jaguar/iguana monster, devouring human bodies.*

Pages 2–3: *Temple of the Five Stories (on right) and Platform of the Knives (on left), Edzná, Campeche.*

Pages 4–5: *Detail of a Flower Mountain mask from a stuccoed frieze, Balamk'u.*